PLACES OF PILGRIMAGE

Ian Scott Massie

First published in Great Britain in 2015

Society for Promoting Christian Knowledge
36 Causton Street
London SW1P 4ST
www.spck.org.uk

British Library Cataloguing-in-Publication Data
A catalogue record for this book is available from the British Library

ISBN 978–0–281–07518–8
eBook ISBN 978–0–281–07519–5

Typeset by Graphicraft Limited, Hong Kong
First printed in Great Britain by Micropress

eBook by Graphicraft Limited, Hong Kong

Produced on paper from sustainable forests

Dedicated to the memory of Paul Nash:
the constant companion I've never met.

CONTENTS

INTRODUCTION

Come with me.

Stand at the edge of England where the sands stretch across to the tidal island of Lindisfarne. Walk the sea-damp causeway until you find your feet once again on firm ground. Here the breeze weaves through the spiky, grey-green marram grass; birds hang in the salt air, riding the wind. Keep still, listen, look . . .

Can you feel it? That spirit of place?

In certain locations, the mix of invisible and tangible aspects, utterly unique and deeply cherished, move us in a manner we find difficult to explain. Our memories are filled with such places, and when we dream, these are the special locations we return to. Reading a book or a poem, our minds build on images of landscapes, villages, cities, shorelines filled with meaning: a day on a childhood holiday; a walk where we sensed the first leanings towards love; the street that suddenly felt like home.

The extraordinary thing is that many of us gravitate towards the same places. With some, the attraction is obvious, such as a breathtaking view or a heart-stopping waterfall. But often the magic is unexpected, generated simply by a certain path, a clearing in a wood, the top of a hill seemingly undistinguished from all the surrounding peaks. Some of the locations in the paintings and screen prints contained here are places of pilgrimage in the religious sense. In Southwell, for instance, there was a sacred spring, while in Durham the earth refused to set free the coffin of St Cuthbert. The place came first; the religion came later; the pilgrims followed – and found something of that initial, urgent, vibrant sense of somewhere special. Even if religion has abandoned these spots, in many instances that sense remains.

Other images included in the book portray places with old roots, like the stones of Avebury or Men an Tol, or places which have only revealed themselves more recently, like Laurie Lee's beloved Slad or Dylan Thomas's Laugharne. Some have been known to me for a long time and have huge personal significance; others I have found in the process of making these pictures. Throughout, I have felt the constant presence of fellow travellers, each of us going in the same direction, drawn by the same emotional, spiritual pull.

Working on this book has been a wonderful journey and the best thing about it is that the pilgrimage isn't over . . . There are always more extraordinary places to explore.

—

On a misty morning, with its elegant towers rising above the fenland fields, the lush trees and the mellow houses, Ely Cathedral – the Ship of the Fens – does indeed bear resemblance to a great stone galleon.

The EAST of ENGLAND

CAMBRIDGE

The outskirts of Cambridge looked much like those of any city. Traffic lights and bungalows, mock-Tudor semis and parked cars . . . I followed the road towards the centre on this my first proper trip, with hazy memories of being here as a teenager. But it seemed a long time ago, and this time my senses were sharper.

I parked on Queen's Road where the broad paddocks stretch across to Trinity College. It was like strolling through a country meadow as I took the path that led to the River Cam until, on a small bridge, I stood and gazed at that iconic stretch of water. Punts glided beneath trailing willows against a backdrop of mellow stone colleges – like warm, grainy footage of an old travelogue.

Entering Cambridge between the high walls of Trinity Lane, I discovered that by great good fortune I had found my way into the heart of this beautiful city by the loveliest route.

On my right, the ethereal majesty of King's College and the tower of Great St Mary's Church. Along the road to my left, the gatehouse of Trinity College and the Round Church. This short half-mile of astonishing architecture, from the elaborate gilded beasts of St John's to the half-timbered perfection of Queen's College, captivated me. It still does.

But Cambridge wears her jewels lightly. The atmosphere, even when this street is at its busiest, is relaxed. Shadows span the narrow spaces, sun falls on warm stones and bicycles of every vintage glide between the buildings.

Many people strive to come here: to study where their heroes have studied, to benefit from the huge well of knowledge deepened over centuries, to tread the hallowed boards of the university's famed Footlights Society, where Fry and Laurie, Mitchell and Webb, and so many Pythons and Goodies have learned their trade.

For me it is a place for browsing in bookshops, for lingering over a coffee, for picking up a pencil and sketching a Georgian cupola, a Baroque pediment, a Tudor tower. If you are an architectural pilgrim or an artist, Cambridge is close to heaven.

Queen's College, Cambridge

BLAKENEY POINT

On a muddy creek, bordered by acres of salt-water reeds, is Blakeney Quay – a grand name for a few planks of weathered wood, green with seaweed. We're gathered here for a trip to Blakeney Point, a shingle spur which almost closes off the entrance to the harbour. As our blue and white, low-sided boat waddles through the creek and out into deeper water, the chug of diesel becomes part of the background, for everyone is watching intently for their first sight of a seal.

Every so often the heads of these wonderful creatures, which look like aquatic Labrador dogs, break the water. And as the boat turns the Point and the open sea comes into view, suddenly there are seals everywhere: basking on the shingle, flopping across the pebbles, splashing in the shallows. They are beautiful animals, gracefully turning around the boat, moving at speed through the green water, their big eyes gazing as they pause to watch us watching them.

For a little while we're enchanted, delighted to be out of our element. This lovely place always seems to be bathed in sunshine ... There is a tangible feeling of disappointment when the time comes for us to journey back to real life, leaving the magical beasts of Blakeney Point behind.

Blakeney Point

FLATFORD MILL

I think of John Constable as a genius. There are very few artists who manage to paint nature as it is, but he did. When you get up close to his work, it isn't in the least bit photographic. There are stabs of colour, the sweeping curves of brush marks, spatterings of white oil paint and always, somewhere, a point of burning red pulling the foreground towards you, while the cold blue of the cloud shadows pushes the sky away.

He practised hard. His watercolours and oil sketches start small then get bigger and bigger. For some of his six-footers he made six-foot sketches, so by the time he began the final stage of a painting, he was relaxed, he knew his lines, and he just had to paint the picture that was in his head.

A lot of what he portrayed he knew well. Flatford Mill belonged to his dad and it became the centre of a series of works including his most famous picture, *The Hay Wain* – or, as Constable called it, *Landscape: Noon*.

The Hay Wain was painted in Constable's London studio from a full-scale sketch made with a palette knife. The sky, the trees and the water all have the colour, the movement and the light of a Suffolk landscape, yet there is a looseness to the whole composition which relaxes the viewer. It's a remarkable piece of work.

In the painting are echoed Constable's comments on his Suffolk home: 'the sound of water escaping from mill dams . . . willows, old rotten planks, slimy posts, and brickwork, I love such things.'

Much of Flatford, including Willy Lott's Cottage, which features in *The Hay Wain*, remains unchanged. The trees are different, but they're just the children and grandchildren of the originals.

And people still come here. Not only to visit the scene of his great composition, but also to paint. An unassuming group of buildings by an unremarkable river. But, as Constable has shown us, there is beauty here. Just look.

Willy Lott's Cottage, Flatford Mill

ELY CATHEDRAL

Ely Cathedral is blessed with a charismatic second name: the Ship of the Fens, which conveys pretty well the way the great Norman church seems to float across the flat lands of Cambridgeshire. On a misty morning, with its elegant towers rising above the fenland fields, the lush trees and the mellow houses, it does indeed bear resemblance to a great stone galleon.

Some cathedrals have been designed and built to a medieval formula. You can almost hear the master mason mutter: 'You want one of these central towers, a couple of these transepts, and three . . . no, maybe five of these lancet windows,' and so on. But some cathedral builders simply tore up the conventional rule book and did their own thing. Like at Ely.

The Norman cathedral was to be a replacement for an earlier church containing the shrine of St Etheldreda. The builders started with the best of intentions, following the usual patterns, but soon got the message that these weren't going to work. So when the central tower collapsed, instead of replacing like-for-like, they built a beautiful and unique octagonal lantern, decorated with the most gorgeous vaulted and painted wooden roof.

Off to the side of the north transept, a large Lady Chapel was constructed and extensively adorned with carved stonework. Although much of this was subsequently damaged during the dissolution of the monasteries – on the orders, it is thought, of the bishop, Thomas Goodrich – what remains is very impressive.

Indeed, the whole abbey is a riot of colour, a visual feast, from its dynamic geometrical floor patterns to the exuberant decoration of its organ pipes. Surrounded by the tranquil streets of its little city, it is an amazingly uplifting building.

Ely Cathedral

The proper way to arrive at Greenwich is by water. Only from the river do you sense the purpose of this town, with its glorious Naval College, high-sited Royal Observatory and forever becalmed Cutty Sark.

LONDON

WESTMINSTER

When I was a child, I imagined that Birdcage Walk – the road from Parliament Square to Buckingham Palace – was festooned with cages of songbirds hanging from the trees. Memories of watching the pelicans on the lake, listening to the pipes and drums of the Scots regiments on Horse Guards Parade, and gazing at the ruined shell of the chapel at Wellington Barracks are equally treasured. There is something very special about this area from Big Ben to Buck House, which has been utilized by royals and politicians to great effect.

Let's look back to find out why. The River Tyburn bubbles up in Hampstead and runs through what would become the West End, before splitting into two channels to join the Thames. In the middle of the marshy ground where it met the great river was Thorney Island, which would become a very important place. The only major appearance the Tyburn makes now, after flowing under Buckingham Palace, is in forming the lake in St James' Park.

Thorney Island became the site of an abbey in the eleventh century. A royal palace was constructed next door, where the Houses of Parliament now stand, and the abbey was substantially rebuilt a few times to give us Westminster Abbey. Initially the site of Edward the Confessor's shrine – a major draw for medieval pilgrims – the abbey does not just specialize in royal tombs, as would be expected, but is the burial or memorial place of vast numbers of dead poets and ten twentieth-century martyrs. It is also home to the wax effigies once carried at royal funerals: here you can come face to face with Edward III (1377), Henry VII (1509), Elizabeth I (1603) – and a whole candle factory of others.

Across the park looms the façade of Buckingham Palace, another rather strange place. The original palace pointed the other way, facing the gardens; what is now regarded as the front was remodelled in 1913 and a forecourt created by building the railings well away from the palace walls. The road leading to this royal abode was turned into a red carpet in the early 1950s by adding iron oxide to the tarmac. It sounds as if a terribly contrived mish-mash might have resulted, but the funny thing is that it works.

Many's the time I stood across from the palace holding my dad's hand to watch the changing of the guard. The sudden absence of traffic, the red 'carpet', the punch of a brass band in the bright sunshine, the antique uniforms of the Brigade of Guards . . . together, these gave the experience a dream-like quality, as though reality was suddenly suspended.

My own family contributed to the pageantry/pantomime (depending on your viewpoint): my granddad gilded the railings, and he and my uncle also did a bit of work on the Coronation Coach. Whatever you feel about the monarchy you can't help but admire their stage management!

Misty Day,
Westminster

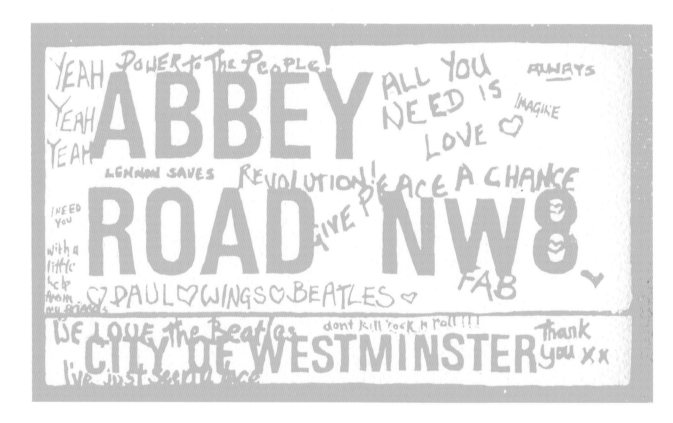

ABBEY ROAD

It's just a zebra crossing on an unremarkable street in north London. Here, while working on the last music they would ever make together, four young men walked across the road a few times while a man on a stepladder took some photographs. So much has been read into the final image: why was that VW placed just there? What did the presence of the police van signify? Why was Paul wearing no shoes? In the studio a few yards away, a handful of years before, the Beatles had recorded their first album in one extraordinary day. It changed their lives. And a song they released 12 months later, as it happened, changed mine. 'She Loves You' made me want to be a musician, a calling I embraced enthusiastically, and when I hear that song now it still pours through me like electricity.

People come here all the time. They have their photographs taken, scribble some graffiti on the road signs and stand by the studio gates, just like hordes of fans used to do in the 1960s.

A famous film-maker once described scriptwriting as 'making nests for magic to happen in' and that's what the Gramophone Company did in 1931 when it opened this place. It made a nest and wonderful, amazing, inspiring magic happened here. Still does. Even if musicians can't afford the studio rent to make an album, they will come from around the world to master their tracks, to imbue their music with some Abbey Road magic.

It's basically a run-of-the-mill town house, built in the 1830s, with a few vital alterations, but from Edward Elgar and Pablo Casals to Pink Floyd and the Red Hot Chili Peppers (who had their snap taken on the crossing too, wearing only socks), Abbey Road is (in the words of Eddie Cochrane) something else.

Abbey Road

HAMPTON COURT

For an enormous palace, Hampton Court is really a parcel of small pleasures. You walk up to the amazing Tudor gatehouse and, while your first impression is of a cliff of mellow brickwork, within seconds your gaze falls on one of the heraldic beasts or an intricately shaped chimney. The complex Tudor clock alone is enough to hold you up for some time. Installed on the gatehouse in 1540, it shows the phases of the moon, months of the year, signs of the zodiac, high tide schedule and, more conventionally, the time. And it's only got one hand!

There is more to get absorbed in here than any other royal palace I can think of, and do you know why? Because the Royals haven't bothered living here for two hundred years. As George III (aka Farmer George, the Mad King) was far happier at Windsor, he began the practice of allowing faithful old retainers and the like to stay here in 'grace and favour' apartments. Hampton Court was thereby spared the makeovers perpetrated on Windsor Castle and Buckingham Palace by successive monarchs over the past couple of centuries.

Hampton Court is really two palaces. At the front is the Tudor mansion that Cardinal Wolsey built in 1514 before giving it to Henry VIII in 1525. (This generous gift didn't save him in the end, but he had the good sense to die before Henry could order his execution.) At the back is Christopher Wren's masterpiece, commissioned by William and Mary in 1689. Wren's initial plan was to demolish the Tudor building but fortunately there wasn't enough cash in the pot to do this. Instead, he joined his English Versailles to Wolsey's palace and created something wonderful.

I've been wandering around Hampton Court since my mum brought me here when I was a small boy, yet I never tire of its wonderful treasures: the maze (of course), Henry VIII's indoor tennis court (still used), the vast Tudor kitchens and – my favourite – the vine. This last item was planted by Capability Brown in 1769 and is the largest of its kind in the world. It lives in its own extensive glasshouse, pleasingly gnarled and very big: 12 feet round the base. Its greatest spur is 120 feet long and it has produced an astonishing 845 pounds of grapes in a season.

There is one thing, however, that I've never seen here, although not for want of trying: a Cardinal spider. The name arises from Cardinal Wolsey's arachnophobia, and the species can grow to be $5\frac{1}{2}$ inches across. One of these days, probably when I'm idly studying a slab of linenfold panelling, I know our paths will cross!

The Great Gatehouse, Hampton Court

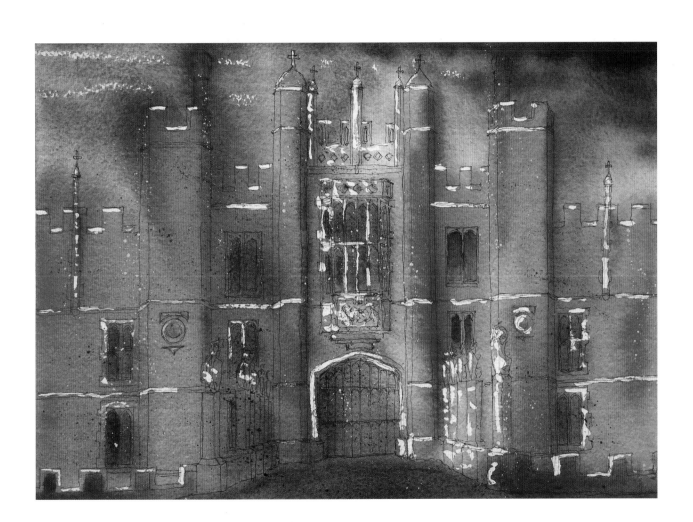

KING'S CROSS STATION

For many years King's Cross Station was a prime example of a beautiful building horribly neglected. Once a wonder of the railway age, it was lost behind clumsy extensions, while the frantic traffic of Euston Road polluted its golden yellow brickwork to a dull grey.

The station stands where London used to dump its rubbish in enormous mountains. (They're portrayed in *The Great Dust Heap,* a striking watercolour at the Wellcome Library, and also appear in Dickens's *Our Mutual Friend.*) So it was probably with great relief that Londoners saw this area cleared to make way for the terminus of the Great Northern Railway. It was built by Lewis Cubitt, whose elder brother Thomas turned the enormous Grosvenor Estate from an unappealing marsh into the richest real estate in the capital. Their younger brother was Lord Mayor of London: a high-achieving family indeed.

Lewis's design for the station was a lesson in functional modernity: two curved-roofed train sheds, a yellow-brick façade reflecting their shape, and the whole thing topped with a clock tower – a physical statement of 'this is where things happen ON TIME'.

My own involvement with King's Cross began early, as this was where we would catch the overnight sleeper to Aberdeen. After being picked up from Fulham in a taxi (normally an unheard-of luxury), we would have our luggage trundled to the train by a porter. Before we set off, my father would indulge me in a walk up the platform to say hello to the engine – which on one memorable occasion was *Mallard,* the big blue record-breaker now in retirement in the National Railway Museum. On board, I would get drowsy as the train chuffed through Potters Bar and past the bulk of Alexandra Palace. The next morning, I usually woke at Waverley Station and watched Edinburgh Castle glide by before the exciting rumble over the Forth Bridge.

King's Cross is rich in stories. There's a long-standing belief that Queen Boadicea lies buried beneath one of the platforms, and her ghost is said to haunt the tunnels under the station. Several movies have featured the building, notably *The Ladykillers,* where the dastardly Professor Marcus plans his audacious robbery. And in *Harry Potter,* the junior wizard is frequently seen pushing a luggage trolley through a wall to get to the magical Platform 9¾. Fans can now have their photo taken with Harry's trolley, which has been artfully half-buried in a bricked-up entryway. Of course, King's Cross has also been the scene of a thousand small dramas of heartbreak and separation, arrival and joy.

The greatest element in the station's recent transformation is the vaulted roof installed on the west side. With a span of 52 metres, the steelwork rises as a central column before splitting into a vast fan which arches and curves down to floor level.

As in all the big termini, there is the feeling at King's Cross that, somewhere beyond those black, mysterious tunnel mouths, something wonderful might just be about to happen.

King's Cross Station

KEW GARDENS

There is a moment in *Breakfast at Tiffany's* when Audrey Hepburn, talking about the eponymous jewellery store, says: 'Nothing very bad could happen to you there.' And that pretty much sums up how I feel about Kew.

The minute I step from Kew Green through those delicate iron gates, a feeling of calm descends. Ahead lie a lot of plants whose names I never remember (although I always read the little plaques), a lake with enormous fish that will take bread from your fingers, greenhouses that look like palaces, and a pagoda. The gardens are not only enchanting but a real force for good. From Kew's scientists have come treatments for malaria and key developments in the rubber industry. In 2012 alone, they came up with 14 new sources of an indigo dye, a medicinal tonic from the sap of a Thai tree and 15 new species of palm.

I have two favourite places here.

The first is the Palm House by Decimus Burton and Richard Turner, built in 1844. A pleasingly bulbous erection of cast iron and curved glass, it is a great place to be on a winter's day. You walk through a fragrant forest of dripping, succulent leaves and musky scented soil. It's like travelling from west London to the Amazon in the turn of a door handle.

The second is the incomparable Pagoda, which stands 162 feet tall and is made up of ten diminishing storeys. Constructed in 1762, it was one of 17 buildings commissioned by Princess Augusta from William Chambers, who came up with a wonderful pseudo-Chinese fantasy. The original decoration was lavish in the extreme: the Pagoda was clad with varnished iron plates of various hues and adorned with 80 golden dragons. But it's had a chequered history. The dragons were sold off to pay some of the Prince Regent's gambling debts and, extraordinarily, the building became a wartime research facility. In 1940 the Royal Aircraft Establishment cut circular holes in the centre of each floor and installed a sandbox at ground level. They then dropped bomb casings from the top floor to test and develop their designs. In 1945 they repaired the holes and gave the building back to Kew.

Kew always brings back memories of my mother. We would come here when I was very young, and a few years before she died it was the setting of one of our last outings together. I'm sure the place means just as much to many other people.

The Pagoda, Kew Gardens

THE WINDMILL, WIMBLEDON COMMON

Certain buildings cast a spell, fire the imagination, inspire the artist, the poet, the storyteller – and nothing quite does the trick like a windmill. Don Quixote jousts with one. Frankenstein's monster perishes in another. Paris's most famous cabaret takes place behind the striking Art Deco façade of the Moulin Rouge, or 'red mill'.

The construction on Wimbledon Common is a perfect addition to a much-loved green space. Its history is simple: it stands as a symbol of the triumph of the people over the aristocracy.

In 1816 a carpenter from nearby Roehampton, Charles March, applied for permission to build a windmill. This was granted and the mill was constructed. It was stopped from working, however, in 1864 when the Lord of the Manor, Earl Spencer, decided to enclose the Common. (He argued that the land was subject to 'noxious mists and fogs' and in addition 'great nuisance was caused by gypsies' who camped on the Common.) This did not go down well with a number of people, including some of the local residents. More importantly, it displeased a Parliamentary Select Committee who were investigating the condition of open spaces around London. In 1871 the Wimbledon and Putney Commons Act was passed, establishing a group of conservators – some elected, some appointed – who would care for the commons.

Wimbledon Common was saved and the windmill remained. It was restored in the 1890s, had new sails in the 1920s and was disguised with dark green camouflage paint during the Second World War.

I loved picnicking beside it when I was a child, windmills being a bit thin on the ground in Fulham, where we lived. Of course, the Common has since become famous as the home of Tobermory, Tomsk, Great Uncle Bulgaria and the rest of the Wombles. It's also turned up in *Doctor Who*, so you may frequently find pilgrims hoping to surprise a Womble or Whovians visiting the site of a favourite episode. Baden Powell wrote some of *Scouting for Boys* when staying in the mill house, and these days it's a museum where you can go and learn how a mill used to work. It's a fitting adornment to a lovely place.

Windmill, Wimbledon Common

GREENWICH

The proper way to arrive at Greenwich is by water. Only from the river do you sense the purpose of this town, with its glorious Naval College, high-sited Royal Observatory and forever becalmed *Cutty Sark*. I loved coming here as a child and I still get a thrill alighting from the boat. Though encircled by one of the world's great capital cities, when you set foot here you find yourself surrounded by little shops, a glorious market and pubs that would be at home in any village street.

What is it that makes Greenwich so special? I think any of the above-mentioned would be reason enough to come, though I do also have a personal connection: Greenwich power station, that mothballed relic of another age, is where my father worked for a time in his days as an engineer with London Transport.

Let's start with the *Cutty Sark*, that elegant tea clipper. As a child I had the feeling I had just missed something, because the *Cutty Sark* was still afloat two years after I was born. If only I had seen her in the water where she belongs! Now she sits in a dry dock only a handful of yards from the river, but it's a journey she will never make. Nonetheless, the way in which the ship, beautifully restored after a disastrous fire, has been encased in flowing waves of glass makes it look as though she is moving while perfectly still.

Leave the ship and stroll through the architectural perfection of Christopher Wren's Naval College and under the colonnades flanking the Queen's House. This confection in white by Inigo Jones was commissioned by Anne of Denmark, the wife of James I, and begun when the Tudor palace of Greenwich was still standing on the Naval College site. James (who reigned from 1603 to 1625) is said to have made a gift of the manor of Greenwich to Anne in apology for having sworn at her in public. (Apparently she had accidentally shot one of his favourite dogs on a hunting outing.) So in 1618, Anne set superstar designer and architect Inigo Jones the project of coming up with a quiet pavilion, suitable for a retreat from the melee of public life, which would (and this is where it gets interesting) double as a bridge over the Greenwich to Woolwich road, so Anne could move between the park and palace in privacy.

The Queen's House, Greenwich

Jones designed the lower half of the existing building (the upper rooms were added later), and the bridge element became redundant when the road was eventually moved. After that, the colonnades were constructed to connect the building with the college. It remains a gorgeous little place, and Anne's insistence that her private abode must retain a river view explains the gap that separates the two halves of the Naval College.

Now climb the hill. The Royal Observatory, commissioned in 1675, was established to expand the nation's knowledge of the heavens and to solve the problems posed by navigating the world's oceans. In time came the establishment of the prime meridian, Greenwich Mean Time and accurate timekeeping. With a nod to this last function, the observatory is topped by a red ball on a vertical slide which was constructed in 1833. Ships in the Thames would wait for the moment when the ball was released at 1 p.m. to set their clocks, and the ball still drops at the same time every day. The Greenwich meridian, which marks the zero degree starting point of the imaginary longitude lines that divide up the sailor's world, is marked across the courtyard. Within the Observatory are John Harrison's clocks (which feature in Dava Sobel's wonderful book *Longitude*), amazing constructions of brass, copper and jewels which first guaranteed accurate timekeeping at sea.

For me, however, the most wonderful thing among Greenwich's embarrassment of riches is the view. As you stand by General Wolfe's statue (a suitable spot for the hero of the Heights of Abraham), a breathtaking panorama of London stretches before you. The river, the towers of Docklands and the distant City spread out like a seventeenth-century engraving. I can't think of anywhere else with so much history, so many stories, so many personalities in one place. It's intoxicating.

Greenwich

THEATRE ROYAL, DRURY LANE

I wouldn't be here if it weren't for Drury Lane Theatre. On this site, where four theatres have stood since 1663, William Wallace Massie, an engineer from Aberdeen assigned to Royal Naval gunnery repair in the London docks, met Lilian Ivy Young, temporarily a sergeant in the ATS, in the closing months of 1939.

When war came, the theatre was turned over to the organization created to bring entertainment to the armed forces: the Entertainments National Service Association or ENSA (aka 'Every Night Something Awful'). Along with other London theatres, it opened its doors not to plays but to dances, and that's how my parents came to know each other – gliding across the floor to 'In a Shanty in Old Shanty Town'.

Like many romances forged in wartime, theirs culminated in marriage only when the war was over. Dad survived the Blitz on London's docks only to be relocated to Birkenhead in time to experience the bombing of Merseyside. Mum worked in a crowded basement in Knightsbridge between stints of fire-watching on the roof. Both emerged determined to make the world a better place by voting for the creation of the Welfare State in the election of 1945.

Sadly they are both long gone, but I stand on the theatre steps and imagine how they walked through those doors, separately, strangers, just part of a crowd – and came out again arm in arm, together. Someone once remarked he had been very fortunate in his choice of parents. I certainly was.

Theatre Royal, Drury Lane

The
MIDLANDS
and WALES

The Chapter House was created by artists whose fingerprints can be found all over Europe. In Lincoln and York they honed their skills before coming to Southwell to execute this magnificent tour de force. Here they reached the zenith of their craft . . .

LAUGHARNE

I was 18 when Dylan's magical words first crossed my path. I had been faintly aware of his poetry in anthologies at school, though we hadn't been properly introduced. However, when my English A-level went badly, I was enrolled at Slough College to have another crack at the exam – and found the syllabus included a collection of Dylan Thomas's poetry and prose. From the first few lines, I was in love.

His words echoed softly and continuously in my mind – the seashore, the tides, the sun on fire through winter trees, the whole sensual landscape of South Wales – in waves of songs without any tune I knew.

Forty-three years later, I stood on the edge of the salt marsh at Laugharne and followed in his footsteps, first to his writing hut and then to the boathouse where he had lived with Caitlin, his wife. It was a glorious autumn day: the ragged cliff of the old castle shining, the winding channel of the river running silver between the headlands.

If ever there was a perfect place for a poet, this must be it. The little town, which became Llareggub in *Under Milk Wood*, is like a stage set – from the curving façades of its coloured cottages, to the grey church where a bright white cross records Dylan's death (on my first birthday), to the sun-hazed sands.

With his words, then and for ever, in my mind, I passed my exam and was accepted by a Durham college. Dylan Thomas enriched my songs, my poetry, my imagination and my life. And it all grew from this wonderful place.

Sir John's Hill, Laugharne

SHERWOOD FOREST: THE MAJOR OAK

Saturday afternoon, just coming up to teatime, anywhere in England, 1955–60.

After the interminable boredom of the football results (followed by the screwing up and flinging on the fire of pools coupons), a little bit of magic used to happen. There was a horn fanfare, the sound of an arrow embedding itself in a tree, then a song would begin: 'Robin Hood, Robin Hood, riding through the glen . . .' For 144 episodes, Richard Greene (Robin), Archie Duncan (Little John), Bernadette O'Farrell (Maid Marian) and other assorted Merry Men carved the legends of Sherwood Forest into my infant brain in stunning black and white.

So it was with a little trepidation that I left the muddy car park, walked past the visitor centre café and set off in search of what a Woodland Trust poll of 2014 revealed to be England's favourite tree. The paths were very tidy and I was far from alone, but it was a beautiful Sunday morning and a heart of stone would have been required not to delight in the long views through the forest. By the time I reached my destination I was feeling very mellow indeed, and there, propped up on substantial supports, was Robin's oak tree. It really is lovely – a mass of branches corkscrewing away from an enormous trunk, dappled light falling through its foliage, deep green shadows in the depth of its leaves.

There are, of course, information boards: weight 23 tonnes, circumference 33 feet, branches spread 92 feet, zzzz . . . More jolly are the targets set up for future Robins and Marians to play bows and arrows, the people walking dogs and enjoying ice creams. And of course it doesn't matter if this happens not to be the actual oak, for the legend is all around us: in the depth of the trees disappearing into the green shade, in the narrow paths that wind off to Friar Tuck's chapel and the Sheriff's castle, in the birds warbling the same songs as their medieval ancestors.

Important trivia: Dick James sang the theme of the TV series and later made a fortune as the Beatles' publisher. The track was produced by George Martin, who produced virtually all of the Beatles' records. And the future star of *The Good Life* and *Yes Minister*, Paul Eddington, played Will Scarlett in 44 episodes of the TV show.

The Major Oak, Sherwood Forest

SOUTHWELL

Southwell is a town pretty much in the middle of England, with elegant houses built around a gem of a cathedral. It has a wealth of stories and history and yet, curiously, it remains relatively little known.

This was a medieval place of pilgrimage. A small, dusty upper room, now the Minster library, was home to a relic – a saint's head. The room has one staircase leading up for pilgrims and another leading down, so there must have been heavy traffic at one time! Here too, in 1646, at the nearby Saracen's Head, King Charles I spent his last night of freedom before surrendering to the Scots at Newark and beginning the long walk to the scaffold by way of his trial at Westminster Hall.

The cathedral town is where the Bramley apple was first grown. From a single tree, which Mary Ann Brailsford planted as a seedling in 1809, came the fruit which has a staggering 95 per cent share of the culinary apple market. But Southwell's greatest glory is to be found within the walls of the Minster.

You approach along a dark corridor which would once have been open and bright. The dimness, the stone passage and the illumination from a series of small stained-glass panels heighten the drama as you eventually turn into the Chapter House. This high octagonal room is awash with bright light from the tall clear windows. Being fairly small, it needs no central supporting pillar, such as in Wells Chapter House, which intensifies its luminosity. The glory of this room, however, is in the detail.

Crisp foliage decorates each stone canopy where members of the church would have met to discuss their business. Hops, buttercups, vine leaves, hawthorn, oak and maple are all here, their leaves scaled up or down to give an appearance of uniformity, while a closer look reveals every carving to be distinctly and gloriously different. Everywhere there are surprises: a hare pursued by hounds, a regiment of 'green men', birds half-hidden in bushes of stone, and a wonderful ceiling boss bursting into leaf.

This room is a great place too for sitting and thinking. Distanced from the rest of the Minster and from the world outside, it is a fourteenth-century space offering heavenly peace, a cave carved from the Nottinghamshire countryside, fossilized for ever. Let the light and the echoes of the Minster wash over you as you drift, meditate, lose yourself . . .

The Chapter House was created by artists whose fingerprints can be found all over Europe, especially in Bamberg and Rheims. In Lincoln and York they honed their skills before coming to Southwell to execute this magnificent tour de force. Here they reached the zenith of their craft before retirement, plague, injury, fashion – who can know? – stopped them taking another step closer to perfection.

Vine Leaves, Chapter House, Southwell Minster

UPPINGHAM

Uppingham is a small, pleasant town with a venerable sixteenth-century school in its midst. But the wonder of the place for me is the Goldmark Gallery.

It was when I was delivering a painting to a local shop that I first stepped through the gallery's door, intrigued by a sign which promised an exhibition by Henry Moore. Now Moore's work normally fetches up in major art establishments like the Tate or the Yorkshire Sculpture Park, so I was curious. It turns out that the Goldmark hosts a constantly changing array of art which would be an adornment for any major gallery. And all for sale.

Mike Goldmark describes himself as a 'shopkeeper', a charming understatement which says much about the Goldmark's atmosphere. His staff are friendly, knowledgeable people who are happy to answer any question you may have, look up information for you in their extensive reference library, or find obscure catalogues from the vast archive. Any art historian would be in paradise.

I come back here time and time again and always leave buzzing with inspiration. Whether you're a lover of the work of John Piper and Paul Nash, like me, or a fan of Graham Sutherland, Eric Ravilious or any of the other stars of the past hundred years, the Goldmark Gallery is a treasure trove.

The Market Place, Uppingham

WENLOCK EDGE

From Much Wenlock to Craven Arms, the mysterious limestone ridge of Wenlock Edge runs for 19 miles, shrouded in trees for much of its length, rising high above the surrounding fields. The Edge was an ocean reef 425 million years ago and the limestone is packed with the fossils of ocean creatures and plants. It was formed south of the equator before the turning of the developing earth landed it in what is now the West Midlands.

The beauty and strangeness of the Edge have inspired a long succession of writers, artists and musicians: A. E. Housman, Ralph Vaughan Williams, L. S. Lowry and Adrian Henri among others. It is magical to lose oneself in the green depths of its steep slopes, and then to climb again to a panorama of the long views across Shropshire.

At its north end is the lovely little medieval town of Much Wenlock, where you can find beautifully preserved half-timbered houses, the impressive ruins of Wenlock Priory and an ancient guildhall.

The whole area feels rooted in an old, old England, and the Edge itself retains the atmosphere of a wild wood where the modern world has never intruded.

Wenlock Edge

STAMFORD

I first stopped at Stamford for the same reason Turner did when he dashed off his famous painting of the place: we wanted a break from the Great North Road. There was a time when the main highway between London and Scotland went straight through Stamford and this, coupled with the town's access to the North Sea via the River Welland, put it in a very sweet spot.

By the thirteenth century, Stamford was one of the ten largest towns in England. It was home to a castle, 14 churches, two monasteries and four priories; occasionally, at least, parliament would meet there. Spared during the Civil War, it prospered through the wool trade and was fortunate to have its Georgian splendours preserved by being bypassed, first by the railways, which discouraged the development of industry round about, and second by the A1 (modern incarnation of the Great North Road), which now thunders past a mile to the west.

The result is that the streets of Stamford and the lovely meadows at its heart are quiet and calm. A host of churches break the skyline with towers, pinnacles and a monumental broach spire. The vast pile of Burghley House hovers on the southern edge of the town. And everywhere you walk you find a coordinated symphony of mellow stone, crooked roofs of handmade tiles, and chimney pots of every fashion. You will have seen Stamford several times as it's been a location for many films and television series: *Middlemarch, Pride and Prejudice* and *Bleak House* among others. It is a study in Georgian civility.

Stamford from the Meadows

The
NORTH-EAST
of ENGLAND

Newcastle is the heart of the North-East and the Tyne is the heart of Newcastle. The crossings are magnificent, from the Victorian splendour of the High Level to the beautiful and functional Swing Bridge.

HEXHAM

Rising above the dale of the River Tyne, the market town of Hexham is a pleasing mixture of building styles: Georgian town houses, Victorian shops, cottages and cafés, churches and chapels. There is a fourteenth-century gaol, a fifteenth-century gatehouse and, at the town's heart, an ancient abbey. Whether you climb up into the town by the lane from the car park or approach it from the heights of the surrounding hills, you get a sense of orderly calm. The town may be threaded with tiny alleyways, but it feels neat and tranquil. And it has a history as rich and satisfying as a fruit cake.

Etheldreda was an East Anglian princess and, later, Queen of Northumbria. She had the difficult task of telling her husband that she had taken a vow of perpetual virginity – something which must have put a bit of a damper on their wedding night. However, as part of her dedication to Christ, she gave a grant of land at Hexham to St Wilfrid, Bishop of York, in 674. Wilfrid set to, building a great abbey that included an extensive crypt and a gorgeously carved bishop's throne. (Fortunately the Romans had departed two hundred years previously, leaving plenty of worked stone lying around in the shape of Hadrian's Wall.)

Another two hundred years later a Dane by the name of Halfdan Ragnarsson burned the place to the ground.

The Normans rebuilt the abbey, and when Henry VIII dissolved the monasteries it became the parish church. There was further rebuilding at the beginning of the twentieth century with a complete reconstruction of the nave.

What has emerged from this long saga is a place with an incredibly rich web of connections to the history of Northumbria. Down in the crypt, Roman stones with inscriptions still visible line the walls. The rood screen and the chancel contain a rich cycle of medieval paintings on wood. Set into a niche in a wall is a tiny ancient chalice. Standing in the north transept is St Acca's cross, carved with knotwork and symbols, the grave marker of an eighth-century abbot. For me, however, the greatest jewel in Hexham's crown is a block of stone known as the Frith Stool – a bishop's throne which has survived from the Dark Ages. It may be that which Wilfrid created for the first abbey, and to touch its delicate carvings is to make contact with the fingertips of the carver who shaped this stone over thirteen hundred years ago.

Hexham Abbey bridges past and present. Beyond its streets, the Roman wall, the border castles and the hills made for walking stretch away to Scotland and the Durham dales. It feels like the ancient centre of a deep-rooted kingdom.

Evensong, Hexham

BARTER BOOKS, ALNWICK

I love second-hand bookshops . . . the smell of old leather, the dust of gently mouldering paper, the light coming in through windows that were last cleaned when George Formby was a rising star. I love the chance discovery, which could be anything from the slim catalogue of a favourite artist's forgotten exhibition, to an out-of-print monograph on some aspect of local history, to an early edition of a famous poet's first work. The only drawback to these temples of discarded words is their lack of methodical shelving. So when I heard about Barter Books and its monumental scale, my first thought was, 'It'll take for ever to find anything!' How wrong could I be.

Alnwick has a beautiful railway station, sitting on a rise across from a monument featuring one of the Percy family's peculiar lions (the tail sticks straight out, since you ask), and this is where the shop is situated. The foyer is full of coffee-table books; the booking hall has a feast of crime fiction; and the platforms are lined with rare first editions, including sections covering gardening, travel and everything else the Dewey system comprises. The trains are long gone (except for the high-level toy one which circles the room where you pay for your purchases). The genius of this place is that it is as beautifully organized as a well-kept library. There are comfortable chairs for sitting and reading, a great café and an atmosphere of serenity.

With its castle, triangular market place of small shops and museum dedicated to fishing tackle, Alnwick is a lovely place. Just off the Great North Road, it's close to the sea and close to the hills, and there can be few better places to curl up with a good read on a rainy day than in Britain's best bookshop.

Barter Books

O western wind

LINDISFARNE

My first trip to Lindisfarne was made at the behest of an accountant from the north-eastern village of Seaton Delaval. His daughter, a fellow student of mine at Durham, had invited me to stay for the weekend, and her father made it his business to ensure that I went away convinced that the county of Northumberland was the finest in the realm.

Driving along the coast road, we passed fishing villages, picturesque ruins and broad, beautiful, empty beaches. Eventually we came to the fairytale castle of Bamburgh and there, across the glittering sands, lay the Holy Island of Lindisfarne.

You motor carefully across the causeway (which is only accessible at low tide), past the refuge on stilts (for unwary drivers trapped by the incoming sea), and pass through the sand dunes into a kind of paradise.

Nothing can prepare you for this place which is more than the sum of several sublime parts. There's the light from the surrounding sea; the silhouettes of castle and priory; the wind tugging at your sleeve. From here Dark Age saints set out to convert the heathen; into this bay sailed the Vikings on their first assault on Britain; within these ruined walls, a lone monk created the heart-stoppingly glorious pages of the Lindisfarne Gospels.

I can never fully express my gratitude to that generous accountant, and over many years I have certainly matched his missionary zeal in introducing others to this magical island.

Lindisfarne Castle from the Priory

DURHAM

One day early in 1973, I got off the train and walked down the long slope of Station Approach towards Durham bus station. I was about to fall in love with a building, but I didn't know that yet. The buses were bound for strange-sounding places: Crook, Pity Me, Hetton-le-Hole. I took the one for Neville's Cross. I was on my way to an interview at a teacher training college – long-haired, restless and almost surgically attached to my guitar. Since leaving school two years earlier I had worked in a market garden, a textile mill, a metalwork shop, a French chateau and on a delivery van. Now I knew what I didn't want to do and had a faint glimmer of what my career path might be. Ten years later I drove away from Durham, still trying to find my way, but with a firmer grasp of the compass and a knowledge that part of my heart would always be in this remarkable place.

The promontory high above the great meander of the River Wear is magical: a collection of beautiful buildings encircled by beautiful trees with the most beautiful cathedral in the world at its centre. I've been painting this place for forty years and I'm not done yet.

The cathedral and castle are the heart of Durham. So much has happened here. This was the place where St Cuthbert's coffin rooted itself to the earth, and where his shrine became a pilgrimage centre behind the high altar of the cathedral. Here his coffin was opened and examined a number of times over the centuries to view his uncorrupted body. And in the treasury, you can see his original, beautifully carved coffin, gold pectoral cross and the stole presented to him at the shrine by King Aethelstan.

Elvet Bridge, Durham

The cathedral commemorates both wonders and tragedy. There is the dark wood and safety lamp of the miners' memorial with its inscription for 'those who work in darkness and danger'. At the west end stands the beautiful Galilee Chapel – where the great Bede lies buried among wall paintings and gilded prayers – which was nearly destroyed by the Georgian celebrity architect James Wyatt before a preservation group intervened. Most poignantly there are the damaged tombs in the nave – a legacy of the terrible mistreatment of the Dunbar Martyrs. (Five thousand soldiers were captured by Cromwell's forces in 1650. On a forced march to Durham two thousand died; another fourteen hundred died in the cathedral itself.) The desperate captives, deprived of food, drink and water, burned what wood they could find but spared the great clock in the north transept that bore the carving of a thistle. It is not surprising that this is a place of enormous spiritual power.

I return to Durham whenever I can: to linger on Prebends' Bridge and gaze at the cathedral, to walk the curving, cobblestoned Bailey, to stroll through the Close, to stand in the Galilee Chapel or, best of all, to climb to the roof of the tower. Durham Cathedral feels wonderful, deep, real. It has wrapped its shadows round me when I've needed comfort; it has held me in streams of refracted light when I've felt joy; it has waited patiently for me to order my thoughts when I've needed space to think. It is a place of sanctuary, standing a little outside of the world. It is a friend.

Durham from Prebends' Bridge

MORPETH

We were sitting in a lively Italian restaurant in Morpeth, enjoying
our ravioli, pizza and asparagus, when my godson turned the
conversation to Emily Wilding Davison and suggested
we find her grave.

Emily's memory is preserved for eternity on a few feet of celluloid
that show her final moments. The occasion is the Derby of 1913. A
group of racehorses sweep into view, she runs on to the track and
is cut down by the flying horses. Whether Emily meant to be
martyred under the hooves of the king's animal or whether she
was simply trying to pin on a suffragette flag, we will never
know. She died in furthering the cause of votes for women.

Her body was brought to her family's grave in the churchyard of
St Mary the Virgin, Morpeth, in Northumberland. The tomb is
quite a grand affair with railings, an obelisk and a plaque. And
on the railings visitors tie the white, green and purple ribbons
of the Suffragette movement to decorate her resting place
and commemorate why she died.

From 1918 some women were allowed the vote, and ten years later
all women over 21 were granted the right. As we stood with the
last light of the April evening filtering through the surrounding
yews, that grave felt like a place of triumph – a symbolic spot
confirming the difference that one person can make.

The Market Place, Morpeth

The NORTH-WEST of ENGLAND

There is a stained-glass window dedicated to those of the Fell and Rock Climbing Club who died in the First World War, which includes that lyrical opening from Psalm 121: ' I will lift up mine eyes unto the hills from whence cometh my strength.'

CONISTON WATER

If you mention Coniston to anyone of a certain age, the name 'Campbell' will soon come to mind, for the place and the name are eternally linked by a few feet of grainy film footage. Donald Campbell was the son of Malcolm who, in 1939, piloted his hydroplane – *Blue Bird K4* – down the lake of Coniston Water in Cumbria at an extraordinary 141 miles per hour. Malcolm Campbell was a tough act to follow. A soldier and pilot in the First World War, he became a motoring journalist and racing driver before turning to the challenges of conquering the world land and water speed records. It is virtually impossible for a man in his line of business to die of natural causes, but in 1948 he managed it.

The words most often used describe poor Donald are 'haunted' and 'doomed'. It is often said that he was the son of a distant and dismissive parent who set out to win his father's love by emulating his success. But Donald endured a career which was one long struggle. His record attempts, which often succeeded, came in the face of technical problems, bad weather and bad luck – particularly bad when *Bluebird K7* leapt from Coniston's waves on 4 January 1967 at something around 320 miles per hour – and sank. The shock was profound. Like Kennedy's assassination in 1963, Campbell's death was captured on camera and endlessly replayed. As he perished, disappearing from view with his teddy bear mascot Mr Woppit, he triggered an outpouring of public affection and sympathy that still accompanies any mention of his name. This tends to mean Coniston Water is perceived as a gloomy place, which is a pity because there are few more beautiful spots in the endlessly beautiful Lake District.

Coniston Water

My wife and I came here on our honeymoon in a borrowed VW camper (see the passage on Grizedale for more of this saga). Driving from Ambleside, the road rose and fell between forests and hills, with tempting glimpses of the Langdale Pikes along the way. Just before the small town of Coniston, we found ourselves descending to a flat valley floor, where the fields were divided up in that traditional Cumbrian way by sheets of stone set on end to form fences. And as we turned towards the eastern shore, what a view! Straight down the five miles of Coniston Water. As the narrow road wove beside the lake, we passed signs and house names – Monk Coniston, Tarn Hows, Bank Ground – and John Ruskin's splendid house of Brantwood. It overlooks a small, enchanted garden, where signs implore you to close the gate to keep the rabbits out. (This is the land of a certain blue-jacketed arch-criminal created by Beatrix Potter, remember.)

Ruskin's reputation has suffered over time, but he deserves to be remembered as a passionate art critic who championed J. M. W. Turner, the Pre-Raphaelite Brotherhood, environmentalism and the preservation of Venice. He must have been a fascinating man, but if that isn't enough reason to visit his lovely house, let me tell you that the tea-room serves meringues as big as your head. With cream.

Pilgrims of all kinds come to Coniston: Campbell and Ruskin fans, climbers, walkers, meringue lovers, beer drinkers (the Coniston ales are superb) and honeymooners. The lake is brighter, more open, than Ullswater, quieter than Windermere, and overlooked by the Old Man, one of Cumbria's loveliest fells.

The Old Man of Coniston

STOCKPORT VIADUCT

Constructed of 27 arches, each with a span of 63 feet, Stockport Viaduct rises 111 feet above the River Mersey. It is 2,200 feet long and took 21 months to build from the laying of the first stone in March 1839. The viaduct originally comprised 11 million bricks (and now, after additional building, 20 million) and cost £72,000.

When I look at the viaduct, I see the paintings of L. S. Lowry. He loved this colossal edifice, and it sails majestically through many of his landscapes, weaving above ponds, mills, houses, churches and people.

Lowry was a man who defied definition in a world that loves to put everyone in a pigeonhole. He was a 'provincial painter', but his work was shown in Paris and bought by the Tate Gallery early on in his career. He was a 'Sunday painter' but, taking account of the quantity of his canvases, must have put in far more hours at the easel than as a rent collector. He was 'an outsider', yet he was represented by a London dealer and elected to the Royal Academy.

He developed a particular delight in confounding journalists by telling stories that appeared to confirm their prejudices, only to come out with a contradictory story to the next reporter who asked the same ill-considered question.

His sublime paintings are the result of a determined effort to find his individual voice, and in this he was much helped by the tuition of a French Impressionist – Pierre Adolphe Valette. Drawing inspiration from Valette's techniques (which included a working knowledge of Monet's and Van Gogh's painting styles) and with an eye to Pieter Bruegel the Elder's busy compositions, Lowry portrayed the energy, humour and tragedy of life in industrial Salford and Manchester, with a pared-down palette of five colours. He also painted searing portraits of desperate people, minimalist seascapes, stylized Pennine landscapes, ships, engines, cripples – and much more.

He was a great man who couldn't be defined in a simple headline and he captured the truth (and the Stockport Viaduct) on canvas and paper in a language of shape and colour that was quite unique.

Stockport Viaduct

GRASMERE

William Wordsworth was a walker. He thought nothing of nipping up Scafell Pike for a picnic when in his seventies. As he was quite content to spend virtually his whole life striding from one place to another, it was fortunate he managed to carve out a job for himself as landscape poet. He happened to be born at the right time, 1770, just as artists and writers were setting off to capture the savage grandeur of nature in paint and words. In the process, they turned the Lake District into a tourism hotspot.

Wordsworth lived for a long time, and when he passed away at the age of 80 he had sadly suffered the indignity of falling out of fashion. While Keats's and Burns's early deaths meant their stars shone ever more brightly, Wordsworth passed from being an *enfant terrible* to being seen as a spent old duffer. He did, however, put Grasmere firmly on the map.

The village is frequently chock-a-block with visitors and yet it somehow rises above this indignity through sheer strength of character. The church is remarkable: a squat fortress with a strange interior of ancient beams and sturdy arches. The graves of William Wordsworth and his wife Mary, his sister Dorothy and various other members of the family lie grey, sombre and dignified beneath overarching yews. On a more light-hearted note, the tiny shop selling waxed paper packets of Sarah Nelson's mouth-watering gingerbread is wonderful: I sometimes draw curious glances from the customers by standing in the doorway simply to breathe in the scented air. The Heaton Cooper Gallery, named for the work of a superbly gifted family of painters, has an amazing selection of art materials: where else can you buy ox gall fluid, tubs of iron filings and Chinese ink stones? And Sam Read's bookshop is a treasure house of literature. (Be sure not to miss the terrific children's section!)

But Grasmere's fame begins with William and Dorothy Wordsworth. Their house, Dove Cottage, is a tiny, cosy gem, with dark panelling, bright fires in black-leaded grates and a small garden. You can feel inspiration drifting through the air with the scents of wax polish and coal dust. It makes you want to sit down at William's desk, flip open a notebook, dip your quill in ink and come up with something like:

Earth has not anything to show more fair . . .

Spring, Grasmere

GRIZEDALE FOREST

In 1968, the Forestry Commission launched a surprising and rather wonderful initiative: it created the Grizedale Society, a body to further the arts in a vast and very beautiful forest. If you take the narrow road that climbs away from Hawkshead in southern Lakeland, you will leave behind the holiday lets and guesthouses as you wind upwards towards a tree-lined crest. At the summit the view opens out dramatically and there is Grizedale, a valley full of thousands of trees, gentle green hills, tiny villages and glittering streams. Into this idyllic landscape, over the past half-century, have come some of the best sculptors from Britain and beyond. Using almost exclusively the materials to hand – timber, stone, clay and peat – and drawing their inspiration from the history of the land, the legends of the woods and the place of humankind in nature, they have created a vast body of astonishing work.

My first view of Grizedale was through the windscreen of a borrowed VW camper van on the day after my wedding. I had suggested we come here for our honeymoon – possibly the second-best decision of my life after my choice of soul mate – and my wife and I were about to be enchanted. It was the beginning of a long and happy relationship with the forest.

Many of the artists who have worked here have deliberately made sculptures which will decay and be as beautiful in that gradual process as they were in the first moments of creation. Wild boars hewn from broken branches and mud peer at you through dappled clearings. Hilltops are crowned by green earthworks. Plantations are measured out in winding walls of dry stone.

Like every funded project, the Grizedale Society has occasionally sailed through stormy waters. Hard decisions and sacrifices have had to be made, and yet the original vision endures. For me the place is wrapped up with memories of the love of my life, of perfect days spent with my children and friends. In Grizedale, magic feels at home. It is both a dream and a wonderful reality. If you've never been, go now.

Grizedale Forest

FIRBANK FELL AND BRIGFLATTS

High on Firbank Fell, near Sedbergh, is a walled graveyard where a chapel once stood. Just outside the wall is a rocky outcrop, marked with a plaque, known as Fox's Pulpit. The Pulpit commands a great view: the Howgill Fells, the Lakeland mountains and south to Lancashire and Morecambe Bay.

George Fox, the founder of the Quaker movement, was 28 in 1652 when he saw a vision on Pendle Hill. He recalled in his autobiography:

> As we travelled we came near a very great hill, called Pendle Hill, and I was moved of the Lord to go up to the top of it; which I did with difficulty, it was so very steep and high. When I was come to the top, I saw the sea bordering upon Lancashire. From the top of this hill the Lord let me see in what places he had a great people to be gathered.

With divine inspiration unmistakably ringing in his voice, Fox came to Firbank Fell a few days later and preached for three hours to a congregation of 'Seekers' – a Westmorland sect in search of an alternative to conventional worship. His sermon marks the beginning of the Quaker movement, the Society of Friends.

Within a few years, the Quakers were a major nonconformist religion and their beautiful 1675 meeting house at nearby Brigflatts stands on the site of one of their first regular meetings.

It's thought that the term 'Quaker' may arise from a court appearance by Fox when he had been charged with blasphemy. He told the magistrates to 'tremble at the word of the Lord'. The presiding judge, a certain Justice Bennett, is supposed thereafter to have referred to Fox's followers as 'Quakers'.

Brigflatts Meeting House is a study in calm and simplicity. A narrow lane of high hedges leads to a cluster of mellow stone buildings and a small, tree-hung graveyard, with green hills rising beyond the surrounding fields. Through the stone arch is a room of plain wooden benches, dark beams and broad windows. The light sifts through the still air, washing the pale walls. Birdsong drifts in from the small garden. This is a place to sit and think, to talk quietly, to move within and without one's being. A sign on the wall declares: 'Thou shalt decide for yourself.'

Fox's Pulpit, Firbank Fell

HADRIAN'S WALL

When I went to Durham to learn how to be a teacher, the college (to their great credit) took us all for a few days out. They reasoned that many of us would be from far away and a sense of educational responsibility, combined with the pride that north-easterners have in their corner of the world, meant they wanted to show us round.

Like all British schoolchildren I had learned about Hadrian's Wall. English children absorb the message that the Scots were ungovernable and savage and best left out of the Empire. Scottish children learn that the Scots were unconquerable and proud of it. Historians, however, point out that neither England nor Scotland existed when the wall was built, rendering both points of view somewhat redundant.

Although much of the wall has disappeared, either becoming the foundation for a road or being buried beneath the city of Newcastle, more than enough exists to amaze and fire the imagination.

The Roman Empire created the wall as a controlled border. (The actual edge of the Empire fluctuated northward as far as the Antonine Wall between the Forth and the Clyde.) Hadrian's project was a huge logistical triumph: 80 miles long, 10 feet wide, up to 20 feet high, with small 'milecastles', major forts, defensive earthworks, customs posts, bathhouses, temples and forward forts north of the wall. It was a major statement about the power and organization of the Roman Empire, one that reverberates still. However, it is in the mind's eye that the wall really comes to life . . .

When W. H. Auden wrote 'Roman Wall Blues' he was thinking what we all do when standing at Housesteads, Chesters or Vindolanda: what was it like to leave your warm, sunny, wine-drenched, olive-oil-drizzled homeland and stand looking into a very different kind of drizzle somewhere between Carlisle and Wallsend? That day, what did we students, drawn from the boring, snoring, suburban hinterlands of Slough, Doncaster, Wolverhampton and Leamington Spa, think as we peered through the Scotch mist? We thought: wow, what an amazing place!

Sunset, Black Carts, Hadrian's Wall

WASDALE

A few years ago when our parish church was having a clear-out, a stash of old prints was discovered. Many of them were engravings based on Turner's journeys in the North, and my wife bought one, had it beautifully framed and gave it to me for a birthday present. It shows a waterfall in a rocky landscape and the title *Mossdale Falls*. Now there were several places it could be, but the one that seemed most likely was in Wasdale – a secluded valley in the Lake District and the starting point for an ascent of England's highest mountain: Scafell Pike. We decided to pay a visit.

From our bed and breakfast at Hawkshead Hill, we drove to Coniston and along the contour line above Coniston Water, until the road peeled away from the lake through a landscape of slate, bracken and pine. Many of Cumbria's lakes are warm, welcoming and comely, but not Wastwater, the deepest in England, where the scree-strewn slopes of Whin Rigg and Illgill Head rise dark and cold and the atmosphere is chilling. It comes as a relief to see the tiny cluster of buildings that comprise Wasdale beyond.

After a squelchy walk through a steep meadow we located the falls, which looked exactly as they did when Turner found them. We could have been looking over his shoulder as he laid down the composition in his sketchbook.

We went to Wasdale's pub (it would have been rude not to) and ate a splendid lunch by a roaring fire. One of the hamlet's claims to fame (along with the deepest lake and the highest mountain) is a competition that started as a tribute to Will Ritson: the World's Biggest Liar. Once landlord of the Wasdale Head Inn, Will lived in the dale for most of the nineteenth century. A typical story of his goes like this.

> The people of Wasdale were famed for growing gigantic turnips. They were so enormous that, once roasted, the villagers would quarry into the insides for their Sunday dinners. The remaining shells were so vast that they were then used as shelters for the local flocks of Herdwick sheep.

The competition is now held at the nearby Bridge Inn and attracts tellers of tall tales from around the world. Contestants have included the comedian Sue Perkins and the Bishop of Carlisle.

Before we left the dale we went to see St Olaf's Church, the third smallest in England. There is a stained-glass window dedicated to those of the Fell and Rock Climbing Club who died in the First World War, which includes that lyrical opening from Psalm 121: 'I will lift up mine eyes unto the hills from whence cometh my strength.' Around the church are memorials to those who have lost their lives climbing, both here and far away. And out in the rough grass of the churchyard there are more graves of climbers. One common theme runs through the inscriptions: they died doing something that they loved.

Wasdale

SCOTLAND

Auld Reekie is a city rich in stories. Every street in the Old Town high on the castle rock, and New Town below, seems to hold a dozen tales…

CULLODEN

We were on holiday at Cullen on the Moray Forth, staying in a caravan in a green meadow by a trout stream. My parents were great fans of coach trips so, on every holiday, we would spend several days accompanying a large crowd of strangers somewhere ... My favourite trips were always the mystery tours. You never knew what the day would hold (although Tunnock's Teacakes, ice cream and chips were pretty much a given), but the journey usually led to something wonderful. On this particular fine Scottish summer day of relentless rain we happened to go, not on a mystery tour, but on an excursion to Culloden.

There are moments in history that cast giant shadows, and the battle of 16 April 1746 is certainly one of those. The events of that April morning make miserable reading, for the Jacobite army was exhausted and outnumbered. Their only tactic – a headlong charge – was rendered redundant by 'Bonnie' Prince Charlie's choice of battlefield, and they were kept waiting for the order to advance for an age, while their ranks were scythed down by artillery fire coming at them through a driving wind laden with snow.

This was not a battle between Scots and English (there were more Scots on the Hanoverian side, for a start) but between the old order and the new, between the tribal clan system and constitutional monarchy.

In the months and years following the battle, the traditional ways of the Highlands were brutally suppressed. Young men were siphoned off to fight in the British army and die in foreign wars. And what the Clearances began, the draw of the industrial powerhouse of Glasgow and the rush of migrants to America and Canada continued, until the Highlands and islands became almost empty.

Most battlefields are just farm fields, but a walk on Culloden Moor is different. In 1881 a memorial cairn was built, and at the same time gravestones were planted, marking the burial sites of the various clans. (The local people who had interred them had identified the Highlanders by their clan badge: a sprig of a plant worn on their bonnet.)

What struck home that day was the sense of personal loss felt by many of my fellow passengers. It was gently explained that nearly all of us had ancestors who were directly involved in this event, and I watched as my parents and many others went from grave to grave finding names from their families. Our lives might have been very different if that April day had never come to pass. The air of sadness was palpable.

Culloden Moor

LOCH NESS

The folklore of Britain is littered with giants, fairies, dragons and beasties of every persuasion, but rising above them all, in both the national and international imagination, stands Nessie – the Loch Ness Monster. I doubt even the most flint-hearted sceptic could drive alongside the loch for any time without glancing at the dark water and wondering just what might be hiding down there.

What is so special about Loch Ness? Well, it's a huge glacial lake (23 miles long), set in a gigantic rift which cuts right through Scotland. It is very murky owing to its high peat content and it's 755 feet deep (so you could stand 4½ Nelson's columns in it on top of each other and they wouldn't break the surface).

Nessie's first recorded appearance was on 22 August 565, when he/she/it had an encounter with St Columba. The saint needed to cross the loch, and as he arrived at the shore he found a group of Picts pulling an injured man from the water. It turned out that the poor unfortunate had been intended as the monster's lunch before managing to escape.

Well, Columba still needed to get across so he ordered a follower to strip off, swim to the far shore and row back a boat. The man obligingly did as he was asked, but immediately Nessie (now quite peckish, having missed out on the earlier snack) went in for the kill. Columba raised his hand, made the sign of the cross and ordered the monster to retreat. To everyone's surprise, it did.

After this appearance, Nessie pops up now and again in the historical record, but in the 1930s he (or she) hit the big time. A snap by a chap called Hugh Grey seems to reveal a creature with various appendages, though downgraded by some to be a swimming dog carrying a stick, while the following year the notorious 'Surgeon's Photo' shows either the head and neck of an extinct plesiosaur or – as was revealed to be the truth forty years later – a modified toy submarine from Woolworths (now extinct itself). Since the turn of the millennium there have been numerous photos, videos, sonar scans, expeditions, documentaries and even a *Simpsons* episode about the monster. The quest and the legend go on.

Loch Ness is so huge, so dark and so deep that we are more familiar with the surface of the moon than with what goes on in its waters. It is surrounded by a monumental landscape rich in legends, overlooked by a crumbling castle, and is very lovely indeed. I have been there several times and I would urge anyone to visit if they can. After all, there must be something in it . . .

Castle Urquhart, Loch Ness

THE HEBRIDES

From the lone sheiling of the misty islands,
Mountains divide us and a waste of seas,
But still the blood is strong, the heart is
   Highland
And we, in dreams, behold the Hebrides.
                              'The Canadian Boat Song'

Like a handful of carelessly dropped pebbles, the Hebridean archipelago decorates the Atlantic waters off the west coast of Scotland. The names of the islands sound like music: Arran, Jura, Islay and Colonsay in the south; Eriskay, Benbecula, Uist, Skye in the north. When the rain comes, they disappear from the curving horizon, only to reappear bruise-coloured on a sea of slate or jewel-like in a flash of falling sunlight. For every Scot (and distanced though I am by time, birthplace and language, I have found I am no exception), they exert an emotional pull as unforgiving as a spring tide.

I was caught unawares. For many years, I had almost taken Scotland for granted as a place of childhood holidays (featuring endless days of cold grey rain) where I felt I did not belong. Then one glorious morning, when we were staying at Glenelg on the shores of the Sound of Sleat, I rose early, walked to the bridge over the burn, looked at the morning sun through the birch trees, heard the pull of pebbles on the shore, saw the blue haze of Skye across the water and, with a shock of recognition, felt myself come home. All the songs, stories, poems and pipe tunes that had accompanied me all my life coalesced in the shadow of the Hebrides and made perfect sense.

The Hebrides are complicated. Through the missionary activity of Columba and Aidan, they are where Christianity first spread to Scotland and Northumbria, yet they have long been divided along Protestant and Catholic lines. They are islands where people have been treated like cattle: expected to fight for their chieftain's cause or exported and cleared away for sheep farming. They are places of great beauty where children have left to find work elsewhere, hoping one day to return, only to see their villages colonized by holiday-home owners and priced beyond their means. But there are also many stories of hope, of communities revitalized by finally owning their land and using modern technology for energy, communication and business. And, of course, the islands carry a wealth of history, legends and literature, accompanied by an intoxicating air of romance.

I have made my pilgrimage to the west coast many times since my epiphany and, having once recognized the gold, it shines for me every time.

*The Hebrides
from Sanna*

EDINBURGH: GREYFRIARS KIRK

Auld Reekie is a city rich in stories. Every street in the Old Town high on the castle rock, and New Town below, seems to hold a dozen tales. There's the legend that the Royal Mile follows the spine of a dragon sleeping beneath the rock; the account of the villainous Deacon Brodie who became immortalized in *Dr Jekyll and Mr Hyde*; the chronicle of the brutal murder of David Rizzio in front of Mary, Queen of Scots, at Holyrood Palace. But the story that draws most people is that of a small, shaggy Skye terrier called Greyfriars Bobby.

Before entering the jumble of ornate tombs in the kirkyard of Greyfriars, you pass a lifelike statue of Bobby, sitting on a column on the corner of Candlemaker Row and George IV Bridge. And inside the church gates lies a slab covered with sticks, leads and dog toys – gifts people bring for the little terrier.

Although the story comes in various versions this is the most common one: Bobby was the companion of John Gray, a night watchman who worked for the Edinburgh City Police. When John died in 1858 he was buried in Greyfriars Kirkyard and the faithful dog refused to leave his master's grave. Such was Bobby's loyalty that he stayed with his erstwhile companion for 14 years. He became a celebrity, cared for and fed by the people of Edinburgh.

In 1867, his dog licence was bought by the Lord Provost of Edinburgh, Sir William Chambers (better known as the publisher who created *Chambers Dictionary*). Bobby died in 1872 and lies buried just inside the kirkyard, close to his master. The famous statue was erected a year later, and since then several books and films have immortalized the terrier. He continues to draw far more people than those who come to Greyfriars to see its other great claim to fame – the National Covenant.

The Covenant was a document signed by Scots Presbyterians in 1638 to state their position on the right of any man or woman to order the affairs of the Church of Scotland. Both Charles I and Charles II believed in the Divine Right of Kings which made them infallible rulers and head of the Church of Scotland, but this was unacceptable to the Covenanters. Their document stated that they were answerable to no one except Jesus Christ. From 28 February 1638, when the National Covenant was signed in Greyfriars Church, the Stuart kings were without the support of many Scots who would otherwise have been on their side. The Covenant is often regarded as the first declaration of human rights. Be that as it may, it can't match the pulling power of a wee dog.

Edinburgh from Calton Hill

ARDNAMURCHAN

Like a crooked finger pointing west, Ardnamurchan reaches towards the Inner Hebrides. Stretching out above the Isle of Mull and lit by a lighthouse on its Point, this is a strange and stunningly beautiful part of Scotland. The long, twisting, single-track road follows the coast by the waters of Loch Sunart, where seals, otters, basking shark and porpoises pop up regularly. It feels very remote but that's just an illusion, for the western edge of Scotland was not made for roads and cars – it's a place for boats. The seas are busy with fishing vessels, whale watchers, salmon farmers and ferries of various sizes, connecting the islands along the dotted tracks marked on the map.

There are so many aspects to Ardnamurchan. At the head of Loch Sunart is Strontian (from the Gaelic for 'the point of the fairy hill'), a thriving village despite its lead mines now being inactive, while at the tip is the vast crater of a dead volcano. In between is a landscape bursting with wildlife, where an eagle is always soaring overhead. On the north-west coast lies the bay of Sanna – its silvery sands lapped by a turquoise sea – which looks out to Rum, Eigg and the far Cuillin Hills of Skye. And on the southern side of the granite finger, not far from the tiny harbour of Kilchoan, is Camus Nan Geall, a steep bowl of green hillsides stretching down to a small curving bay. A place of wonders, according to tradition. For the great St Columba once landed here, and having a child to baptize and needing

water, he prayed . . . Immediately a spring came bubbling out of the rock creating St Columba's Well. Indeed, the little bay is awash with history: in the shade of a group of trees are the remains of a Neolithic chambered tomb, and butting up against this, in a mass of grey stone walls and nettles, is an ancient burial ground of Clan Campbell. The gravestones are carved with coats of arms and a crucifixion, and a standing stone has been Christianized with a cross. Around the bay are the tumbled remains of long-empty old houses.

Ardnamurchan has something of the Highlands and something of the Hebrides and a lot of history. It was here that Charles Stuart landed in 1745 before raising his ill-fated standard at Loch Shiel. It was here that some of the cruellest events of the Highland Clearances took place, when the land was swept clear of people to make way for sheep. It was here that strontium (named after the village) was discovered, which helped give us radar, television and nuclear weapons.

For me it will always be a place of calm, of reflection, of inspiration – and that long and winding road is always beckoning me back.

Ardnamurchan Point

ABERDEEN

The granite city, the city of Bon Accord, the most northerly city in the British Empire, the setting of 'The Northern Lights of Old Aberdeen', the 'silver city with the golden sands', my father's home, and the focus of a kind of pilgrimage that happens all over the world.

The Robertsons were a fairly typical Scottish family, living at the beginning of the twentieth century. Neither wealthy nor desperately poor, they decided to seek a better life in America. My grandmother, Isabella Robertson, had married Alexander Massie, a tailor (like Isabella's father) and a man who lived most of his life in debilitating poor health.

When the Robertsons left Aberdeen for New York they realized that, because of his chronic illness, Alexander wouldn't be eligible for immigration.

So Isabella remained with him while 13 members of her family went ahead to begin a new life. For years after, like many ex-patriates, they turned to face Scotland at the end of each day in memory of their homeland. Decades after the Robertsons had become part of their adopted country, a trickle of relatives began to make their way back to the north-east to visit relatives around about.

My father left Aberdeen in the 1930s and my mother's father left there in the 1880s, both drawn to better prospects in London. And so, as a child, I too became used to visiting Aberdonian relatives on summer holidays and being shown the places my father loved.

This is a pilgrimage common to any community which has become scattered for one reason or another. There is somewhere that remains special . . . somewhere we still think of as home.

Memories of Aberdeen, the Granite City

EILEAN DONAN CASTLE

That the work of human hands occasionally joins with nature in creating something wonderful is gloriously borne out by the existence of Eilean Donan Castle. Three sea lochs – Loch Duich, Loch Long and Loch Alsh – meet at the tidal island in the Western Highlands of Scotland, and during major restoration to the castle in the early twentieth century a footbridge was built tying Eilean Donan to the shore.

Donnan was a Celtic saint who built a small church here in the seventh century and gave his name to the rock. The castle dates from the thirteenth century and was home to the Mackenzies, the Macraes and various members of the Matheson clan (possibly ancestors of mine), one of whom could apparently speak the language of the birds.

Considering its miniature size, the castle has enough history to fill several volumes, so I'm just going to cut to its downfall. The Jacobite rebellions did not go well for Eilean Donan. In 1715 the Macraes danced on the roof before setting out for the Battle of Sheriffmuir in which 58 of them perished. Four years later, as 300 Spanish soldiers were garrisoned in the castle (allies of the Scots Jacobites), three Royal Naval warships turned up and battered it into submission before destroying the building with gunpowder.

The castle was rebuilt between 1919 and 1932 by a descendant of the Macraes and, in a land famous for castles, is now the third most visited. Why do people flock to this little jewel? Well, once you have seen Eilean Donan reflected in the loch against the backdrop of the mountains of Kintail, you will know. It is simply perfect. Here, in one spot, come together so many strands of Scottish history: Celtic saint's island, clan stronghold and site of scenes in the disastrous Jacobean drama which brought about the destruction of traditional life in the Highlands.

Eilean Donan Castle

The
SOUTH-EAST
of ENGLAND

Oxford has so many exceptional places: St Mary's Church where the Oxford martyrs were tried; the Botanical Gardens where Will and Lyra meet at the close of Philip Pullman's His Dark Materials stories; the Ashmolean Museum, the Radcliffe Camera, and so on and on. But for me, a little room in the Bird and Baby trumps them all.

TURVILLE

Lying in a deep fold of the Chiltern Hills, overlooked by a picturesque windmill, Turville's enchanting cluster of cottages, church and pub have long delighted pilgrims in search of the perfect village. A favourite location for film-makers seeking to portray an ideal Englishness, it is now also visited by the fans of those movies and television programmes, who are, inevitably, charmed.

I first encountered the village in *Went the Day Well?* – an extraordinary piece of movie-making released in 1942. The Brazilian-born director Alberto Cavalcanti had noted with alarm what was happening in Europe on his way to sanctuary in London. He felt that the British needed shaking out of their complacency in the face of the dire threat just across the Channel, and setting his film in Turville, he got his message – 'this could happen here' – across perfectly. Because of a misplaced trust in authority and in their local squire, a quiet village allows a contingent of seemingly authentic British soldiers (actually Nazi paratroopers) to take over the place. When they finally awaken to the treachery in their midst, the villagers deal with it in a swift and courageous manner.

Most of Turville's roll call of appearances are less traumatic. In *Midsomer Murders, Jonathan Creek, Morse, Goodnight Mr Tom* and *The Vicar of Dibley*, it presents its calm, good-natured and overtly English face to the world.

So a walk in Turville feels strangely familiar, and the expectation of bumping into John Thaw or Dawn French takes a little time to get over. But it is easy to see why it has enjoyed its share of attention. It really is flawless.

Last Light, Turville

BRIGHTON

The Prince Regent liked Brighton very much.
So much that he built himself a modest seaside
property. Of course, being the Prince Regent, it had
to have a certain style and, more importantly, cost
a ridiculous sum. The Brighton Pavilion was the
result, and you know what? I loved this crazy pile
of faux-Oriental architecture, which has every bell
and whistle imaginable, from the first moment
I saw it. It was worth every penny.

Brighton itself is a wonderful town. There used to be
a great time-filling short, which the BBC ran between
programmes, entitled *London to Brighton in Four
Minutes*. They had put a camera in a train cab at
Victoria Station, recorded the journey as seen through
the driver's window, and speeded up the result. It
was like an acid trip for 1950s kids and I thought it
was brilliant. If only the real journey had been
similar. It seemed to take for ever on the dirty green
electric train out of Victoria, past Battersea power
station, through the suburbs and down to the coast.

But when at last we arrived, we made for the
beach. Now the word 'beach' may imply sand,
but at Brighton what you get is a world-class
selection of pebbles on which sitting in comfort
is a challenging experience. The town does have
other delights, though: Volk's Railway, sticky lengths
of pink rock and abundant supplies of ice cream.
And top of the bill must be the Palace Pier. This
was where I first came across a 'What the Butler
Saw' machine – a hand-cranked flip-card film
show featuring antique lovelies in outfits
considered daring in 1923. Marvellous! The pier
also boasted a ghost train, dodgems and slot
machines aplenty. We had nothing like this back
home, and to this day I remain a sucker for a
pier – Southwold, Saltburn, Southend . . . they're
all wonderful.

In my mind's eye Brighton is a sort of Edwardian
theme park by the sea, and although when I
return these days I find myself in the twenty-first
century, the town will stay that way for ever in
my imagination.

Palace Pier, Brighton

CHALFONT ST GILES: JORDANS

In the leafy county of Buckinghamshire, where the beech trees meet over the sunken lanes of the Chiltern Hills, stands a humble Quaker meeting house, its red bricks and handmade tiles blending into the surrounding autumn foliage. Alongside the building, there is a small graveyard – the resting place of William Penn.

Penn's father was owed £16,000 by Charles II. This was a huge sum (about £2 million at current value), and Charles settled the debt by giving the land of what would become the US state of Pennsylvania to William. William set off for America to establish a Quaker colony, which grew into a haven of religious tolerance and in time became home to Scots Calvinists, persecuted Jews, Huguenots, the Amish and a host of others. Penn managed to establish this arcadia while negotiating successful treaties with the resident Lenape tribe. However, life was to be unkind to him and he returned to England to die penniless in 1718.

The Quakers had a tough time when they first emerged in the 1650s. Initially they were persecuted, and it wasn't until 1687, when Charles II passed the Declaration of Indulgence, that they were allowed to build meeting houses.

At Jordans Farm in Chalfont St Giles, four acres were set aside for a burial ground and a meeting room. As early as 1688 the building was up and running, and it is still in use today. The simple architectural style – brick without and bare wood within – reflects the principles of the Society of Friends. It is a space of great peace.

Next door is the Mayflower Barn, a venerable farm building that includes the timbers of the *Mayflower*, broken up at a yard in Rotherhithe. The claim that this was the ship which took the Pilgrim Fathers across the Atlantic has never been proved, as *Mayflower* was a fairly common ship's name: when the famous vessel was afloat, there were at least 37 other *Mayflower*s at sea!

Jordans lies close to the M40 motorway and less than an hour from the centre of London, yet an aura of serenity surrounds you as you sit on the plain benches of this simple meeting house, and the beech trees swish gently beyond the window panes.

Jordans Meeting House, Chalfont St Giles

COOKHAM

In our late teens, my friends and I would occasionally forsake our local in Slough and come to Cookham. The quiet little village by the Thames had (and still has) some nice pubs and a very tranquil air (certainly compared to Slough). We would sometimes sit over a beer at Boulter's Lock on a summer evening and watch the boats gliding up and down the river. It was quite idyllic.

There are many places worthy of inspiring great visionary artists to record them but few are as lucky as Cookham, which had the good fortune to be the birthplace of Stanley Spencer. Just before his arrival on the world's stage on 30 June 1891, a crow slipped down the chimney, flapped its sooty way around the room and then flew out of the window. His parents took this as a good omen.

Stanley was born into an extraordinary family that included two professors, a violinist, a conjurer, and a fellow painter in his brother Gilbert. He studied at the Slade at a time when the school was turning out some of the greatest artists of the twentieth century, and was soon awarded the nickname 'Cookham': he simply never stopped being fascinated by the place he referred to as 'the Holy suburb of Heaven'.

Much of Stanley's work centres on his visions of biblical events set among the houses, streets, churchyard and riverbank of his home village. Although his work includes a number of other masterpieces (and I don't use the word lightly) – the murals for the Sandham Memorial Chapel, the war paintings of the Port Glasgow shipyards, the recording of his obsessive love affair with Patricia Preece – it is in his pictures of Cookham that Stanley achieves artistic greatness and touches our hearts.

To see the residents of the village rising from their graves in the churchyard on the day of judgement, and boarding a river steamer to sail to paradise, speaks to us so eloquently of love that it is impossible not to feel uplifted.

Walk the streets of Cookham where Christ makes his entry into Jerusalem; stroll across the town moor where lovers entwine among the cattle; share Stanley's vision, and be lost in it.

Cookham from the Thames

DORCHESTER ON THAMES

Dorchester is a tiny village. It's been bypassed by the main road,
by changing times and by history, but its roots are deep
and it remains a place of great power.

In 635 Bishop Birinus was sent to England. At Churn Knob, a short
step from Dorchester, he preached to the King of Wessex and, as a
result, a Saxon cathedral was built. Like many other cathedrals, this
was subsequently replaced by a Norman abbey church. Expanded
in the thirteenth and fourteenth centuries, with each development
it became adorned with more remarkable treasures.

But a visit to Dorchester isn't about the sculptural beauty of the
Jesse window or the wonder which is the twelfth-century lead
font. The abbey is greater than the sum of its parts: in the rich,
shadowed heart of this old church there is an invitation to
forsake the material for the spiritual world, and whether
you're a believer or not, you can feel the building
striving to help you cross that line.

Dorchester Abbey

DUNGENESS

Derek Jarman was an artist, a designer and a film-maker. I first saw his work – though I didn't know it at the time – in the amazing sets he designed for Ken Russell's *The Devils*. Russell was always being branded an e*nfant terrible* and, after a while, Derek was too. He was never going to be a crowd pleaser. He had too much to say and he wanted to say it his way, but in the process he created some wonderful films. For my money, *Caravaggio* and *Edward II* stand up well against the work of many highly regarded, but more conventional, film directors. Derek's time passed all too quickly, his life snuffed out by the dreadful disease of AIDS. But then a strange thing happened. Through one small facet of his life's work, he started to become more widely loved in death than he had ever been in life.

Dungeness is a place right on the edge: a shingle spit thrusting out into the English Channel from the mysterious flatlands of Romney Marsh. The further the small road takes you, the more unworldly the land becomes. The shingle is littered with dead fishing boats propped up on crutches. There are rusting railway lines, a distant, incongruous nuclear power station and a straggle of tarred, weather-boarded sheds.

Around one of these is a carefully arranged sculptural garden. Twisted pieces of cast iron sprout like flowers, arrangements of pebbles break up the shingle backdrop and salt-loving plants spread across the stones. On the side of the cottage, its yellow window frames vivid against black walls, are the beautiful lines of John Donne's poem 'The Sun Rising'. This is Derek Jarman's garden.

Although as out of the way as it could be, this tiny house and, more especially, its garden draw visitors from all over the world. Much of Derek's work was about people the establishment regarded as low life – the poor, the gay community, the dispossessed, the alienated – and he made them rich, dignified and beautiful. Here, again, he has taken the flotsam, the rubbish from the shoreline, and laid it out for us, asking: isn't it beautiful? Yes, it is.

Prospect Cottage, Dungeness

RUNNYMEDE

'King John was not a good man', begins A. A. Milne's poem, and he was right. In 1204 John lost the lands of Normandy and Anjou to the French king. He then spent ten years raising money through punishing taxation – and other less legal means – to fund a campaign to win them back. During this period he took hostages, seized lands and castles, murdered his nephew and starved to death the wife of a particularly powerful baron.

The reckoning came in 1215. The barons revolted and forced John to sign one of history's most important pieces of paper: the Magna Carta. This momentous event took place at Runnymede, a leafy meadow beside the Thames in Surrey. Magna Carta included some clauses which went on to establish a host of human rights. Chapter 39 stated that 'no free man is to be arrested, or imprisoned . . . or exiled . . . save by the lawful judgement of his peers or by the law of the land'. Chapter 40 asserted that 'to no-one will we sell . . . deny or delay right or justice'.

Of course, this legislation only applied to earls, barons, bishops and abbots – not to the lower orders and certainly not to women – but human rights had to start somewhere.

Magna Carta has been cited many times: in the state's case against Charles I; in the composition of the American Declaration of Independence; in Nelson Mandela's 1964 trial. Chapters 39 and 40 are still on the British statute books today.

In many places human rights are continually being stamped on, but walking through the lawns and trees of Runnymede is an experience that inspires hope. It may be the incongruity that a great document of state was agreed in a meadow rather than a palace or castle; it may be the beautiful setting – a green field by a broad river bordered by overhanging trees; it may be the eloquent understatement of the Magna Carta memorial and the one nearby to the assassinated American president John F. Kennedy, which is similarly simple in style. Both speak, in their inscriptions, of liberty. Somehow it seems to make sense in this lovely spot.

The Magna Carta Memorial, Runnymede

SILCHESTER

High on a Hampshire hill is a rough pentagon of big old crumbling flint walls. An aerial view reveals it to be the spot where a web of green tracks converge – from London, Winchester, Bath and St Albans. At the height of summer, a pale grid of streets shows through the crops in the fields, and tucked into the eastern corner is a tiny church.

Silchester is one of the best understood of our Roman towns. Unlike London or York it was not built over, which means the archaeology is not hard to get to or difficult to interpret. The place has yielded up a few things of great beauty: carvings of cats and birds, an exquisite horse, gaming boards and lamps.

But Silchester's real glory is its atmosphere. There is a special warmth about this place with its long views over the soft green curves of Hampshire and Berkshire. It is always quiet except for birdsong, and with no artificial light dimming the night sky the stars seem close enough to touch.

The little church was erected where two Roman temples stood and their bricks have been used to make its walls. Outside is a wide pond, home to blue streaking kingfishers and clockwork-striding moorhens. Inside the church, the plaster is decorated with faded 700-year-old wall paintings of flowers. This is where I met my wife, and where my children were given their names. It is perfect.

St Mary's Church, Silchester, Evening

LANGLEY MARISH

When John Betjeman came to sum up Langley church he said it had 'everything a church should have', and so it does. Stained-glass, gilded monuments, a hidden Tudor library, medieval floor tiles – they're all here and as familiar to me as my fingers and toes. This was the church in which I sang as a choirboy and where I passed hours of enforced leisure (while interminable sermons droned on) just looking. Looking at the green man with leaves pouring out of his carved mouth, looking at the graceful chamfering of the window tracery, looking at the monuments to long-dead members of the Nash family around the chancel.

The Nashes remained at the back of my mind until in the school library I came across a picture I liked by Paul Nash. I read a little about him and found he had lived at Iver Heath – just up the road from Langley.

Now graveyards have always been favourite places of mine. They're often the most interesting spot in a town or village, particularly once everything around them has evolved into identikit houses, shopping centres and car parks. In every sense they are a community's most direct link with its past. And one day, when I was walking the overgrown paths

between Langley's host of dead people, I came across a small, grey grave – an upright slab bordered with pillars, in front of which was perched a carving of a hawk which seemed to be reading the words: 'In Loving Memory of Paul Nash, Painter, Designer'. Underneath were the words: 'Whatsoever things are lovely, think on these things'.

So here lay the man who painted the picture, buried in *my* churchyard! After that came many happy days finding more pictures (including one in which the hawk makes an appearance: *Landscape from a Dream*), a sketch and a passage in his biography of *Spring at the Hawk's Wood* – one of my favourite places. Understanding Paul's vision was very easy because I found I saw the world in the same way. Places have personalities and it is possible to portray those personalities in paint, in words, in music.

There are many graves to which pilgrimages are made: saints, monarchs, artists, poets and musicians. Whether it's Karl Marx in Highgate or Jim Morrison in Paris, I suspect they bring a similar measure of comfort, connection and human understanding that I find here. I have been to visit Paul many times, and although the conversations have been rather one-sided, they have often been very important. And I have always felt better as I've walked away.

St Mary's Church, Langley Marish

CANTERBURY

When Thomas Becket was brutally murdered by four knights in Canterbury Cathedral in 1170, his death sent shock waves through Europe. Miracles were soon ascribed to Becket, a shrine was built, a steady stream of pilgrims began arriving and a mountain of wealth accrued. Of course, all this activity ended with the dissolution of the monasteries – or did it?

The fact is that pilgrims still come to the city. It may be to appreciate the magnificence of the cathedral, or to see the spiritual heart of the Anglican Church, or because they have travelled to England from far away and have been told Canterbury is somewhere they simply shouldn't miss.

I am drawn to the place by two works of art. Like many English O-level pupils I had to study part of Geoffrey Chaucer's masterpiece *The Canterbury Tales*: expecting to find it boring, to my astonishment I discovered I loved it. (As did Edward III – he gave Chaucer a gallon of wine a day for life for writing poetry.) A terrific adaptation of the *Tales* was running then in the West End, so off I went to see it, and it was great – full of fun, farts and fantastic stories. The *Tales* are funny, moving, rude and infused with such an understanding of humanity that you cannot help but see yourself in them. The distance of several centuries shrinks to nothing.

The second work which has affected me is the 1944 film *A Canterbury Tale* written and directed by Michael Powell and Emeric Pressburger. (You may also know them as the creators of *The Red Shoes* and *A Matter of Life and Death*.) Powell, who came from just outside Canterbury, and Pressburger, an Anglophile Hungarian screenwriter, created a little piece of magic in their tale of three 'pilgrims' all in search of something. A man with an empty life, a grieving lover and a stranger in a strange land all land up in a Kent village, travel to Canterbury and have their lives transformed. Along the way, the film speaks of the determination to create a better world as the end of the Second World War comes in sight; and like Chaucer's writing, it builds a bridge between those who lived centuries ago and those who live with similar challenges today. Indeed, to walk through the medieval streets and enter the gateway of the Cathedral Close is to be surrounded by a host of fellow spirits, who have shared the burden and blessing of being human.

Cathedral Close, Canterbury

GREAT COXWELL BARN

Looking from the small village of Great Coxwell, you can see the Uffington White Horse riding on its green hill. The older houses here are of honey-coloured Cotswold stone, with roofs which are thatched, hipped and dormer-windowed in a satisfying procession of sizes and styles. Situated in this green vale between the limestone hills and the chalk downs, Great Coxwell is similar to the other small villages round about. But it has an exceptional treasure: an agricultural outbuilding generally regarded as the finest surviving medieval barn in the country.

Beaulieu Abbey in Hampshire, like all medieval abbeys, owned granges (farms on land that had been granted by various benefactors), and one of these was in Oxfordshire, at Great Coxwell. A large grange needed a large barn and this one, built around 1250, is 152 feet long, 44 feet wide and 48 feet high. It is constructed of rough courses of Cotswold stone, its outer walls reinforced with broad buttresses.

'As beautiful as a cathedral,' said William Morris, and, stepping inside, the analogy makes perfect sense. The oak timbers, set on stone supports, rise to hold up a roof of geometrical perfection. The timberwork disappears into shadows unless the broad doors have been thrown open, as they would be when the threshing floor was in use. Then the wind passing through the building would carry the chaff outside and leave the grain within.

The scale of the barn, the receding darkness, the light lancing in through narrow openings – all these contribute to an atmosphere in which the building itself feels alive. This is a place whose stones bear witness to the voices and the rhythmic sounds of generations of labour.

Great Coxwell Barn

OXFORD: THE BIRD AND BABY

There is a pub in Oxford called the Eagle and Child, known to most
Oxonians as the Bird and Baby. Very small, dark and oak-panelled,
it looks the sort of place a hobbit might choose to drink. Or where,
in an upstairs room set on a tilted, creaking floor, there might be
a wardrobe filled with fur coats which, when pushed aside, reveal
a frozen land where it is always winter but never Christmas.

In the cosy back area on the ground floor, there is a plaque that
explains everything. Here is where the Inklings would meet every
Tuesday to discuss and read out their developing stories. The
group's best-known members were Professors Tolkien and Lewis,
authors of *The Hobbit, The Lord of the Rings*, The Chronicles of
Narnia, *The Screwtape Letters*, among many other works. The
shelves are lined with their books. The ceiling is stained with
the smoke of long-cooled hobbit pipes. And the beer,
as one would expect, is excellent.

Oxford has so many exceptional places: St Mary's Church where
the Oxford martyrs were tried; the Botanical Gardens where Will
and Lyra meet at the close of Philip Pullman's His Dark Materials
stories; the Ashmolean Museum, the Radcliffe Camera, and so
on and on. But for me, this little room trumps them all.

Oxford Spires

WITTENHAM CLUMPS

Paul Nash, one of the greatest artists of the twentieth century, grew up close to where I lived as a boy. I explored the nooks and crannies he had known and sang in the choir of the church where he lies buried. And through a developing love of his paintings, I came to know new places. One of these is close to the Thames near Dorchester in Oxfordshire – two low hills, both crowned by trees, known as the Wittenham Clumps. In the first lazy years of the twentieth century, Paul came to stay here with his cousins. However, while the family went off to shoot, he pulled out a sketchbook and a box of watercolours.

This visit opened Paul's eyes to his calling as a landscape artist and a discoverer of the spirit of places. He called the Clumps 'the pyramids of my little world' and their extraordinary presence shines out of his early pictures. Later, as a war artist, outraged at the dreadful suffering of soldiers in the 1914–18 conflict, he articulated his sorrow through depicting mutilated fields and trees.

In the Second World War, Paul sat slowly dying from chronic asthma in an Oxford nursing home. Through a pair of binoculars he could see Wittenham Clumps, and around them he constructed his last great sequence of masterpieces, which includes the muscular *Landscape of the Vernal Equinox* and the lyrical *Landscape of the Summer Solstice*. The hills convey his acceptance of approaching death as the finale of a natural cycle; his vision of the landscape tells the story of his place in the turning universe.

The Wittenham Clumps

The
SOUTH-WEST
of ENGLAND

St Ives has atmosphere, severity,
light, gloominess, terrific charm
and a well-worn beauty as complex
as the taste of a great malt whisky.

THE RIDGEWAY

Few places made such an impression on my young mind as this prehistoric road. Running from Streatley in the Thames Valley to Avebury in Wiltshire, it connects with other ancient routes, most notably the Icknield Way, and has a string of hill forts, barrows and outstanding remains along its route. To walk the long ridge is to walk in the footsteps of our ancestors.

Historians come to this highway to reflect on the days before England existed, and to muse on exactly where Alfred defeated the Danes in the Battle of Ashdown. Poets have composed stanzas walking its ruts of chalk and clay. Walkers rise to the challenge of completing its green length, passing high above the villages and towns which line the downs.

The Ridgeway changed my perception of what a highway could be. Of course, I was aware that the A4, which flowed a few yards from our house, was the Roman road from London to Bath, but now I discovered that, with a few old maps, I could find history in the most surprising places. A lane by the name of Green Drive runs through the Langley council estate where I grew up. I found that it connected the Tudor mansions of Ditton Park (once the possession of Anne Boleyn) and Langley Park (home of the king's forester John Kedderminster and later a country home of the Churchill family). The footpaths which criss-crossed the 1950s estate were there on old Ordnance Survey maps and one, peculiarly raised, had been the track of a wagon way running through the Victorian brickfields.

Thanks to an epiphany on the Ridgeway, I look at every road and path with a questioning eye, and I am still discovering stories in the least promising of places.

The old track where all this began changes little. In spring the grass banks are bright with orchids and alive with bees. Overhead, larks sing, kestrels hover and clouds cast shadows. Occasionally, there floats up the rattle of a distant train down in the Vale of the White Horse. If the soul of this lovely country resides anywhere, it is here.

The Ridgeway

WAYLAND'S SMITHY

The approach to Wayland's Smithy could not have been more wonderful. On an early summer day, with birdsong overhead, chalk underfoot and flowers lining the track, I pushed through the gate and saw the mantle of trees for the first time. Walking through the cornfield was like walking through the mists of time.

Another gate, and I was in a cave of beech trees and looking at the long barrow, a low, grass-covered burial chamber. Every shape seemed perfect – the curving upright grey stones, the bowed grey trees, the patch of blue sky above. Those shapes have called me back again and again.

Wayland, the son of a Norse god-giant, is the subject of a host of stories, but his great claim to fame was his skill as a smith, a job which always seems to border on magic. He was so proficient, and his work so prized, that a vain king captured the smith, lamed him by cutting his hamstrings and put him to work on a remote island. Wayland was having none of this. He killed the king's two greedy sons and made goblets from their skulls, raped the king's daughter and escaped to Valhalla, flying on wings he had forged.

The Norse who came to these chalk downs during the Dark Ages probably connected the long barrow with Wayland because he was also associated with labyrinths. For a long time, it was thought that the tomb chambers were an entrance to such a place.

The best-known part of the legend is that you can leave your horse here in the evening, lay a silver coin on a stone as payment, and in the morning your horse will be shod and the coin gone.

Wayland's Smithy

THE WHITE HORSE OF UFFINGTON

Below the Ridgeway and the green ramparts of Uffington Hill Fort is to be found, in my view, the most beautiful of the hill figures to have survived in Britain. The curving lines of the horse echo the curves of the downs: the body, limbs and head of the creature, cut into the contours above a steep, deep hollow, are abstracted, flowing – more spirit of horse than horse itself. The figure does not feel like an imposition on the land but an entirely natural thing – a white horse on a green hill.

When I arrived at the site for the first time fifty years ago, the climbing road revealed little of the horse itself, and I walked over its vast body without managing to make much sense of its anatomy at all. This obscurity and the blue distances of Oxfordshire sailing away to the north added tremendously to the mystery of White Horse Hill. The low crest of Dragon Hill in the foreground (where St George dispatched the monster and where, poisoned by the monster's blood, the land will grow no grass) and the deep valley of the Manger heighten the drama of the landscape. But find a good viewpoint in the Vale of the White Horse and the loveliness of the gliding, soaring animal is revealed.

It is a great work of art that speaks as eloquently as anything that ever graced a gallery wall.

The White Horse, Uffington

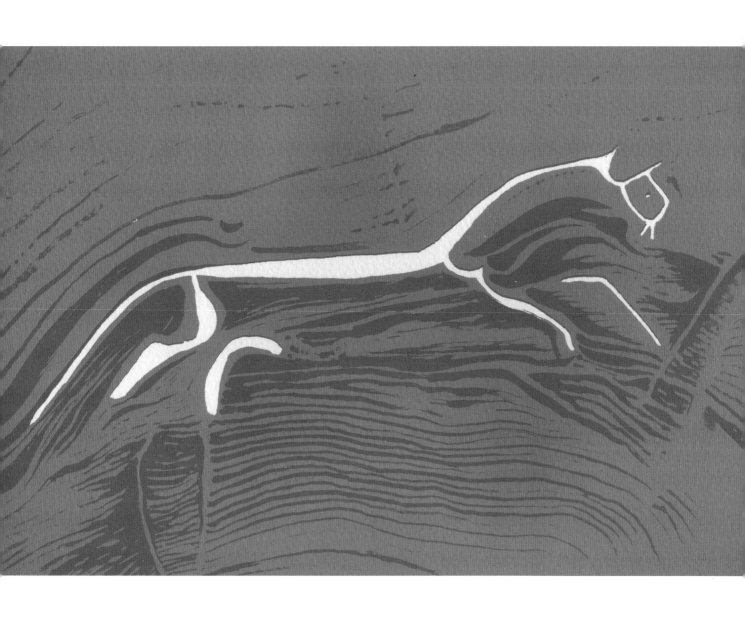

STOURHEAD

The south Wiltshire countryside is rolling, green and adorned with small, tree-topped hills. The overgrown lanes are rich with campion and mayflowers in the late afternoon light. A road leads down, past an ornamental gateway, between steep, ivy-covered banks, underneath a slender bridge. It feels as if we are leaving the real world and entering an enchanted realm, but at last a sort of reality reasserts itself. It's a very soothing kind of reality, however: one made up of a mellow brick pub, a row of comfortably weathered cottages and a glimpse of silver water. There is a courtyard where ice creams and cream teas are being happily consumed and a medieval church. By the entrance to the fabled gardens stands a monumental fourteenth-century market cross, adorned with statues of kings.

The view opens up. In the foreground a bridge, five arches gently rising to a central point, mirrored in the green water. Beyond, a lake stretches to fill the valley and, in the distance, a classical temple stands tethered by its own reflection. Around the water's edge more temples and pavilions, framed in greens and reds by ornamental flowering trees, decorate the narrow paths in the golden, late spring sunlight.

I had read about Stourhead but I had no idea it would be like this. The story is: wealthy banker Henry Hoare commissioned a sublime Palladian house from the famed architect Colen Campbell, but sadly expired the year the house was completed. However, his son, also named Henry, had plans to enhance this masterpiece. His vision was of a landscape comprising carefully composed vistas giving the viewer the feeling of walking through a series of landscape paintings. He dammed the River Stour to form the lake, and surrounded it with temples and trees, here and there allowing the eye to slip away to longer views, linking his 'ideal' landscape with the wider world. He subsequently became known as 'The Magnificent'.

I came here expecting a landscape pruned and trimmed, neat and severe, but around this gorgeous lake wild flowers and grasses fringe stands of ornamental trees. Children run, climb and disappear into sprawling rhododendron dens. Little old ladies (probably carrying concealed secateurs) totter along the gently sloping paths. And, as I stand by the water's edge to breathe it all in, a bride in a cream silk dress and a groom in naval uniform step out of the trees. I feel as if I've wandered into a scene from *Far from the Madding Crowd.*

Stourhead is a place of pilgrimage for that most English of eccentrics – the folly fan. But it's also for children whose memories you want to fill with a vision of loveliness, for weary people seeking peace and serenity, for lovers who want possibly the best wedding photograph location in England.

Summer, Stourhead

MEN AN TOL

Approaching this enigmatic group of stones across the ragged, windblown moor, my first impression was of how small they are. This part of Cornwall, on the Penwith peninsula west of St Ives, is littered with massive quoits, ancient fortresses and standing stones.

But this little group has a magic of its own. Men an Tol is thought to have been part of a stone circle, most of which has disappeared, though this theory has yet to be tested by a complete excavation. A rival theory is that the stones were part of a burial chamber, but I'm afraid, on account of their scale and layout, that I don't subscribe to that one. Over the years they've been damaged by cattle, and recently some twisted soul inexplicably decided to cover them with inflammable substances and set them on fire.

But on the day I found this small cluster of stones, it was the dead of winter and there was no one around. I ran my fingers over the warm, silky granite, knowing I was tracing their contours just as thousands of others have since they were first set upright. The central stone, with its smooth round hole, is where countless people have thrust damaged limbs, aching heads and sick children in the expectation of healing. In truth, there has been so much hope expended here that you can feel it hanging in the air. And I want to trust that a host of people who walked back down the track woke the next day to find that their life was just a little better, if only through the power of faith.

Men an Tol

GLASTONBURY

There are a few places around Britain which really feel as if they are touched by magic, and Glastonbury is one. The cynical and cold-hearted may find it easy to laugh at the many shops run by groovy people selling crystals, yogic charts and manuals for Tuvan throat singing, but they're not here by chance. Glastonbury has a strange and wonderful side to it that is worth a closer look.

Simply approaching the town arouses a feeling of being somewhere special. It stands high above the low-lying Somerset levels, which became a flooded plain about ten thousand years ago. To get around, the residents built wooden trackways through the marsh, and the oldest one found so far is a staggering six thousand years old.

The town first gets a mention in about 700. According to Hugh Ross Williamson, St Collen, one of the hermits then living on Glastonbury Tor, was summoned by fairies and shown a floating mansion of the dead. Using holy water the saint banished the vision, and the chapel of St Michael was later built to ward off such unchristian influences.

The first church on the site of Glastonbury Abbey dates from 650, and its use as a royal graveyard suggests that the place was already seen to be very special. Three early kings, Edmund I, Edgar I and Edmund II, were buried here, and in the twelfth century the discovery of the grave of King Arthur added a fourth royal interment.

Collen and Arthur are by no means the only major figures with connections to the abbey. There is a legend that Joseph of Arimathea – one of the few people to be mentioned in all four Gospels – came here with the young Jesus and provided the inspiration for William Blake's poem 'Jerusalem':

> And did those feet in ancient time
> Walk upon England's mountains green?

This legend gave rise to Glastonbury's alternative title of 'the New Jerusalem'.

Glastonbury Tor

Another story tells that Joseph came here after Jesus' death, bringing the Holy Grail in which he had collected some of the blood of the dying Christ. He is said to have hidden the Grail in the Chalice Well. On this visit he is also supposed to have thrust his staff into the ground, whereupon it burst into leaf. It is known as the Glastonbury thorn and it flowers, appropriately, on Christmas Day.

So this is a place of great legends, but what does it feel like? The first time I set foot here was on a freezing January morning. The frost was a crisp crust of ice through which I crunched to visit the grave of Arthur and Guinevere. In the stillness of the mist everything seemed possible. The washed-out colours and the grey stone, my breath hanging in the air and the distant birdsong all came together with the magic of the place. Yes – it felt very special.

And is Glastonbury Avalon, the fabled resting place of Arthur? There is plenty to suggest that the discovery of his grave here was faked by monks eager to boost their abbey's fame. In any case, Arthur, although he may have been a man, is much more important as an idea. The thought that a hero exists who will return in his people's greatest hour of need is overwhelmingly reassuring. The questing Knights of the Round Table, the great but humanly fallible lovers Guinevere and Lancelot, the wise wizard Merlin forever living backwards through time, are all aspects of a story which, for its depth of understanding of human frailty, is unmatched.

This place feels right. If the Once and Future King lies here awaiting his return, I wouldn't be a bit surprised.

Glastonbury

AVEBURY

Every year our school would arrange for a fleet of grey coaches from the local Windsorian bus company to be lined up along Lascelles Road, ready to take us to a place of 'educational value'. Fortunately my memories of the prickly moquette seats and the faint but characteristic odour of small children have been largely overwritten by the experiences of those trips, one of the best of which took me to Avebury.

To board the bus amid the dull suburban streets of mock-Tudor semis around Slough Grammar School; to get off in the middle of a ritual landscape five thousand years old – it was like a trip in the Tardis! I felt I had left a fake England and found a real one in the small village within the huge 'henge' ditch and stone circles.

The atmosphere at Avebury that beautiful day was beyond words. I felt 'in touch'. I have tried and failed to put it any better than that, through poetry, songs and paintings over many years.

The stone circles are part of a larger ancient landscape that includes Silbury Hill, West Kennet Long Barrow, stone avenues which march through the fields towards the village, outlying monuments at Windmill Hill and the Sanctuary, and a host of round barrows. Here too is the western end of that ancient road, the Ridgeway.

The first historian to recognize Avebury's importance was John Aubrey, who stumbled across the village while pursuing a fox in 1649. He made drawings of the place that turned out to be invaluable because when another historian, William Stukeley, came to study the site seventy years later, many of the stones had gone. After surviving nearly five millennia, they had been systematically broken up by a farmer needing building materials. It was the Dundee marmalade millionaire Alexander Keiller who finally safeguarded Avebury. He bought 950 acres, carried out archaeological surveys, raised fallen stones and created a museum before selling the lot to the National Trust – at agricultural value only.

Avebury still draws me whenever I'm in the area. The spirit of the place is moving, comforting, sustaining.

Avebury

SLAD

Slad clings to the slope of its Gloucestershire valleyside like an alpine village, its houses tumbling in a scatter of Cotswold limestone out of the high beech trees above, and down towards the river below. The road follows the contour line and cuts through the little place between the old school and church, on one side, and the Woolpack pub on the other. It is at once very ordinary and very special.

Slad was home to Laurie Lee and is immortalized in the first of his autobiographical accounts, *Cider with Rosie*, which I have loved most of my life. There are unexpected strands of darkness in his tales of a jumbled family in a chaotic cottage and the small tragedies and joys which beset various members and their neighbours. But the writing is so humorous, beautiful and dazzlingly poetic that I could never tire of reading it.

I visited Slad with my son, also a lover of Laurie's work. We went first to the small, dusty Victorian church and found his grave. Looking across his beloved valley, golden in autumnal sunshine, I was more moved than I could say. His cottage was exactly as described, and the Woolpack seemed just about the most excellent pub I have ever been in (and my research in this area has been extensive). We sat there, surrounded by his books, hearing his words ring in our heads and hearts.

It has been said that Laurie Lee wrote a hymn to a vanished England, but I don't believe that to be the point of *Cider with Rosie*. What he makes me see is that every life – especially during the challenges of childhood and adolescence – is a story worth telling.

Rosebank Cottage, Slad

CERNE ABBAS GIANT

The Giant, sometimes known as the 'Rude Man', is one of the best-known hill figures in Britain. He's big and impressively well endowed. But he's a chap with a shadowy past.

The Giant first gets a written mention in the eighteenth century, which seems a little late because he's pretty hard to overlook, but many ancient landscape features – such as Avebury – were ignored by the writers of books prior to this period. The general feeling, partly based on other archaeological sites in the area, is that the Giant is much older and probably dates from the first couple of hundred years AD.

He's thought to result from an attempt to combine the Greek–Roman god Hercules and a local Celtic deity. A rival story, relating to nearby Cerne Abbey (now in ruins), relates that he is the work of monks making an elaborate comment on the randy practices of their expelled abbot. But it's more likely that the abbey was founded here to Christianize this pagan site.

Why have people come here? The answer is disarmingly simple. Barren women would spend a night alone with the Giant, and couples who were having problems conceiving a child would make love within the enclosure of his enormous penis.

The Giant is in an area of outstanding beauty, even by Dorset's high standards, and sited next to a village which is pretty much perfect. And the strange thing is that he fits in, just like his brother, the Long Man of Wilmington, away over in Sussex. It seems the most natural thing in the world to have a big (180-foot-high) naked man gazing out from his chalk hill, wide-eyed, beautiful and benign.

The Cerne Abbas Giant

CHYSAUSTER AND CARN EUNY

I was staying in St Ives when I read about the existence nearby of an Iron Age village – a small cluster of well-preserved ancient dwellings, in use around the time the Romans were introducing the British to underfloor heating and the correct way to eat figs. So early one morning I set off to have a look.

I am occasionally the butt of jokes when over-punctuality crops up in conversation. If a train is departing at, say, ten o'clock, I'm perfectly capable of hounding everyone to the station for half past eight. So it was no surprise that I got to Chysauster an hour and a half before it opened and was faced by a locked gate. Well, climbing over that was one of the better decisions I've made, because I got the whole place to myself.

Chysauster is a village of houses, each with a courtyard around which is set a number of rooms which would once have been thatched. Each house has a main doorway facing east and a paved entrance. The whole place has a well-planned, secure feeling about it, and I pottered about for some time, finding it remarkably easy to see how the village worked and being impressed by the level of sophistication and the high quality of the building techniques.

Chysauster also has a fougou. This is an underground passage (the word comes from the Cornish for 'cave'), usually open at both ends. Fougous were a feature of several settlements of this era but no one knows what their function was. They don't seem to have been made for defence or for storing food, which inevitably leads to the assumption that they must have been created for 'ritual purposes'. Whatever their function, they have a distinctly strange feeling. The fougou at Chysauster has been blocked up because of safety concerns, but at nearby Carn Euny there is a cracker which runs for 65 feet just below ground level, its roof made up of enormous stone slabs. It has a small chamber off to one side and is believed to have had another entrance at one time. You would think a fougou would feel like an early subway, minus the roar of traffic above, but it's not like that at all. I've been in many underground places – crypts, mines, potholes – but the fougou at Carn Euny is different. You really feel as though you are taking a journey into a spiritual underworld. The passage may or may not have been made for this purpose, but that's the message my senses were sending to me.

Both Chysauster and Carn Euny are on the windswept Penwith peninsula at the very end of Cornwall. It's an extraordinary landscape, full of holy wells, standing stones and early settlements of all kinds. You'll never be anywhere like it.

*The Fougou,
Carn Euny*

DARTMOOR

I've always been a fan of Sherlock Holmes. I first got sucked in by a creaky, black and white television retelling of *The Musgrave Ritual* but it wasn't long before I was devouring Arthur Conan Doyle's short stories, and later on his novels. One of my most prized possessions is an enormous, two-volume, annotated edition of every tale of the great detective.

So the first time I drove across Dartmoor in a tiny clattering Mini in the early 1970s, my heart was aflutter because this was the home of that great Holmesian nemesis the Hound of the Baskervilles. (If this was an audio book I'd insert a blood-curdling howl at this point, but I'm afraid you'll just have to provide one yourself.)

Well, I wasn't disappointed. I don't mean that I was pursued by enormous dogs with phosphorescent jaws, but that the atmosphere was everything I'd hoped for. As I drove across the wild landscape, mists shrouded the craggy heights and a cold drizzle descended from a sky of low clouds.

Dartmoor is huge – 368 square miles – and is home to the greatest concentration of Bronze Age remains in Britain. Scattered across its grey and green acres are standing stones, hut circles and kistvaens – a kind of stone tomb. The area is also rich in folklore. At Fox Tor Mires – the inspiration for Conan Doyle's Great Grimpen Mire – there are tales of the mysterious lights known as Jack O'Lanterns which lure the unwary into the deepest, most dangerous part of the bog. It's sometimes said that these are actually the ghost lights of a tortured soul – an escapee from Dartmoor Prison who, lost and afraid, was sucked down into the liquid peat of the mire.

So my first encounter with Dartmoor was gloriously creepy, but on subsequent trips the weather has always been depressingly pleasant. The place is certainly worth a visit, and not just for Holmes fans, but do wait for a splendidly miserable day before you go.

Breaking Light, Dartmoor

BRADFORD ON AVON

It seems extraordinary that a whole church could be lost and then found again, but that's what happened here. St Laurence's Church has been around for a very, very long time and has remained fundamentally unaltered. It was probably when the Norman parish church was being constructed nearby that it began to disappear – new buildings surrounded it and it stopped being a church. It subsequently had a chequered career as a cottage, a school and a factory. In 1857, however, a clergyman by the name of Canon Jones set out to do some detective work. He had been leafing through the writings of William of Malmesbury, a medieval monk and historian, which mentioned the church existing in the 1120s. With the help of the details of a land grant by King Ethelred to some nuns from Salisbury in 1001, Jones worked out where St Laurence's might be. He found it surrounded by added buildings and lacking its original furnishings, but when everything was cleared away the beautiful church emerged.

It's very high with tall, slim doorways and a pattern of arcading on the outside walls. Stepping inside, you can feel the weight of the years in the cool darkness. High on the east wall are two carved angels which have somehow survived, formal yet lovely in their crisply carved robes. The original chancel arch had been taken down so that a chimney could be put in but, miraculously, the stones had been kept and these were used in the restoration.

Though its population is only a little over nine thousand people, Bradford on Avon is a remarkable place with an astonishing array of architecture. In addition to St Laurence's, it has four Anglican churches and a chapel, two Baptist chapels, a united (Methodist and United Reformed) church, a community church, a nonconformist church, a Quaker meeting house and a Roman Catholic church. Its other gems include a half-Norman bridge with a distinctive lock-up added to its side. This has a weather vane of a gudgeon on its roof, hence the local expression for being in jail as 'under the fish and over the water'. There is also a magnificent early fourteenth-century monastic barn, which is built like an agricultural cathedral.

Bradford on Avon was a Roman settlement (though probably older, being sited at a useful river crossing) but its wealth grew when the wool trade made vast fortunes for some of its citizens from the seventeenth to the early twentieth centuries. It had 30 woollen mills at its peak!

Commerce aside, if you want to know how churches used to feel before centuries of makeovers turned them into stained-glass jewellery boxes, St Laurence's, Bradford on Avon, is a must.

St Laurence's Church, Bradford on Avon

OLD SARUM

A little north of Salisbury, not far from Stonehenge, there is an extraordinary thing: a city that isn't there. Old Sarum sits like an enormous green hat dropped on the landscape. The outer rim is a bank and ditch enclosing where houses and a cathedral used to be, and the crown is the earthwork where a castle stood. You can walk through green banks which were city gates, picnic under trees where walls once stood and climb to a tumbled flint ruin. There is a sense that ghosts are all around you; that time is suspended and a clap of the hands will bring the city back to life. What on earth happened? Well, what happened is the history of Wessex.

About five thousand years ago, some people decided to settle down on top of this blustery hill where two ancient tracks crossed. About two and a half thousand years later on, a hill fort was built. Later the Romans arrived, used the fort for a bit and then left. It stood empty for a while after the Saxons took over this part of Wessex, but, after four hundred years, work began on reinforcing the earthworks: the Vikings were coming. Sometime between the incursions of the Vikings and the arrival of William the Conqueror, the name Old Sarum became Sarisburia – which evolved into Salisbury – and when William's son Henry decided Old Sarum was the perfect spot for a castle, he gave the resulting fortress to the Bishop of Salisbury. Roger, the bishop, built a palace and cathedral below the castle mound. Unfortunately the cathedral lost its tower only five days after being consecrated. It really is windy here!

Old Sarum was always classed as a castle and the monks of the cathedral had to pay rent to the military. Disputes became frequent, and in the early thirteenth century the bishop, Herbert Poore, decided it was time to move. He ran the idea past King Richard and the Pope, who both gave consent, and what followed was a remarkably inspired approach to town planning. The bishop decreed that an arrow would be fired from Old Sarum and wherever it landed they would build their new cathedral. The archer drew his bow, the arrow soared . . . and hit a passing deer. The deer ran for two miles before collapsing by the River Avon, and that is where Salisbury Cathedral was built.

Old Sarum's cathedral was dismantled and the stone taken to the new site. Over time the houses were abandoned and the castle demolished. But a strange legacy lived on. Old Sarum was a 'rotten borough' – a parliamentary constituency controlled, in a shockingly undemocratic fashion, by one person. This empty hill continued to return two members of parliament until the Reform Act of 1832.

Old Sarum draws you in remorselessly. It's a very strange place where the earthworks, walls and gateways speak in the most vivid way. The imagination soars here: it is Wessex's modest Pompeii, cloaked in green trees on a breezy hill.

Salisbury from Old Sarum

TINTAGEL

There is one over-arching legend which finds echoes in every part of Great Britain: the story of King Arthur and the Knights of the Round Table. Arthur's tale comprises a rich group of stories which begin before his birth and then gallop through a complex narrative exploring every shade of human experience: lust, betrayal, faith, pity, murder, redemption, loyalty, laughter and love. The stories have been around for a long time and their origins lie in France, Britain and the imagination of the man who first pulled them all together: Thomas Mallory. He wrote his great work in prison somewhere between 1450 and 1470, translating existing texts and adding his own ideas.

I came to the stories through T. H. White's wonderful book *The Sword in the Stone*, which led me to *The Once and Future King*, and then I discovered Alfred Lord Tennyson's *The Idylls of the King*. Of course, there are also movies and paintings, but some of the greatest ways to connect with these tales is through the landscape.

Our country is littered with Arthurian sites. He lies sleeping under Richmond Castle and under Edinburgh. His Round Table is at Egmont and Winchester. He is buried at Glastonbury and the Eildon Hills. His Camelot was Colchester, Camelon, Caerwent and here, at Tintagel . . .

A walk through a deep valley brings you to the crashing waves of the Cornish coast. High above, on a massive dark granite rock, a ruined castle seems to hang in the air, tethered to the cliffs by a slender finger of land. It was Geoffrey of Monmouth, in his bestselling *Historia Regum Britanniae*, who first set Arthur here, and he chose well, for this place has everything the legend demands. The seas thunder around the vertical walls of stone, filling Merlin's Cave beneath the castle at high tide.

When I arrived on a grey February day, the rock was deserted, and after climbing the steeply sloping bridge I had the place to myself. Of all things, I began remembering the closing scenes of the movie *A Connecticut Yankee in King Arthur's Court*, when Bing Crosby sees Rhonda Fleming, the love of his life whom he thought was lost. I was eight again, on a Sunday afternoon in Slough, watching a film in black and white, and I left the castle humming 'We're Busy Doing Nothing' in a haze of happiness.

Tintagel

ST IVES

On my first visit to St Ives, I had a strange experience that made me question whether I had gone abroad by mistake. Having set off from Yorkshire on a freezing grey January morning, I got out of the car at journey's end and found myself embraced by a warm, almost Mediterranean, breeze, gazing at a turquoise sea. If I had ever wondered what drew artists like Ben Nicholson, Naum Gabo and Terry Frost to this fishing town on Cornwall's toe, I had at least one answer now.

Having grown up in the shadow of the British Romantic School, it was a given that I must make a pilgrimage to St Ives one day. So many artists who had fed my imagination had come here before me or been lucky enough to grow up in this place. Indeed, it is hard to overstate the harbour town's importance to British art. There are galleries galore, often hiding down tiny alleyways, along with Cornwall's own outpost of the Tate. Artists' studios, their rusty window catches rattled by salty winds, inhabit former sail lofts. Visitors can wander through Barbara Hepworth's studio and into her lush, sculpture-strewn garden – a place of pilgrimage in itself. Alfred Wallis's naive paintings of boats, Patrick Heron's dazzling abstracts and Bernard Leach's elegant pots . . . all originate in St Ives. Why find inspiration here rather than, say, Falmouth or Mousehole?

Walk through the town and everything becomes clear, as you take in the beach, the headland, the harbour, the narrow streets and high walls, the granite and whitewash houses that rise and fall as if piled up against the sky. St Ives has atmosphere, severity, light, gloominess, terrific charm and a well-worn beauty as complex as the taste of a great malt whisky. Everything makes the visual senses simply hum with ideas.

St Ives

The Ribblehead Viaduct symbolizes human ingenuity, the power of protest, and the challenges offered by one of England's most breathtaking landscapes. It is a fitting tribute to the Yorkshire Dales.

YORKSHIRE
and the
HUMBER

MASHAM

Like many others, I came to Masham because I wanted to buy a drink. Back then, in the 1970s, Theakston's Brewery had started selling a new cider and a friend and I drove down from Durham to sample a few bottles. We took the A1 south to North Yorkshire, switched to small country roads as the Pennines grew closer and eventually arrived at the edge of Wensleydale. There below us, in the valley of the River Ure, arose the spire of Masham church, with the heather-clad high moors and the folds of Colsterdale in the distance. We crossed the old bridge, passed under an avenue of lime trees and entered the town.

When I saw the market place, it was love at first sight. Here, unexpectedly, was the scale and open aspect of a town square in southern France. There was no traffic, no traffic lights, no plastic shop signs. Just trees around a market cross, a pleasing variety of Georgian houses, a church at one corner and a pub. Perfect.

I live in Masham now, and a lot of people still come here for a drink, calling at either Theakston's or the Black Sheep Brewery. Or for the steam engine rally in July or the Sheep Fair in September. Or to see where scenes from *All Creatures Great and Small* and *Heartbeat* have been filmed. It's that sort of town.

Whenever I've been far away, I like to drive back home down the Thirsk road as I once did on that day long ago. Sometimes mist lies in the valley; sometimes snow lies on the hills beyond; sometimes the surrounding trees are rusty red with autumn colours. Winter or summer, the view warms my heart and I can't imagine I'll ever tire of painting it.

Bright Morning, Masham

SALT'S MILL, SALTAIRE

This is a story in two acts set in a northern mill town. Those last three words may conjure up images of grim smoky skylines, impoverished, broken-backed terraces and dirty, shoeless children. But in fact Saltaire has neat houses, well-ordered streets and elegant civic buildings around a mill which is palatial in scale and style. The town feels comfortable and safe, and my first thought when I came here was: what a lovely place.

Titus Salt, born in 1803, was a man who liked to do things his way. When he started out in the weaving trade, he had an idea that Russian Donskoi wool might improve the locally made worsted cloth. No one showed any interest, so he began manufacturing it himself. In the 1830s, he came across a consignment of alpaca wool and soon became the first maker of alpaca cloth. By 1833 he had taken over his father's textile business, and by 1848 he was the largest employer in Bradford, becoming the city's mayor shortly afterwards.

In 1850, Titus decided to bring his sprawling businesses under one roof and bought three acres of land at Shipley. The result was the magnificent Salt's Mill, which he surrounded with houses, a hospital, a church, an institute and, notably, no pubs. Some have questioned his motives, suggesting what he really wanted was complete control over his employees. But as you walk through the beautiful streets of Saltaire, I think it becomes clear that Titus realized giving people somewhere clean, pleasant and healthy to live would result in a happier, more productive work force.

In time the mill, like so many across the North of England, fell silent. What do you do with something which, when it was built, was the largest factory by floor area in the world? Art is possibly not the obvious answer, but in 1987 Jonathan Silver, a successful businessman and boyhood friend of Bradford-born artist David Hockney, bought the place. A few years earlier he had sold off his business interests to travel the world for a while with his wife and two young daughters.

Silver realized that the huge windows and wide open spaces would be the ideal setting for a gallery. He also created a restaurant and a number of small business units out of the vast building, and today you can buy books, art materials, furniture and high-end designs of all kinds. But the great draw and constant source of delight to visitors and art lovers is the vast amount of vibrant, uplifting work that David Hockney shows on a regular basis.

Sadly, Jonathan Silver died in 1997 and did not live to see Saltaire granted the status of a UNESCO World Heritage Site, which it fully deserves. But he and Titus Salt certainly managed to refute the lie that it's grim up north!

Salt's Mill, Saltaire

SHERIFF HUTTON

Sheriff Hutton is a modest little village. Its single street connects a ruined castle, once the home of Richard III, and a church which houses a rather beautiful but sad monument.

Richard III is a divisive character. Shakespeare made him into one of the stage's great villains, but even during his lifetime there were people who believed Richard had 'a great heart', and it may be that many crimes – particularly the disappearance of the Princes in the Tower – have been laid unfairly at his door. Over the years he has become a sort of historical celebrity, and this cult came to the fore when, in 2012, his body was exhumed from a car park in Leicester. The car park had been built over the site of Greyfriars Church, where the king had been hurriedly interred after his defeat at Bosworth.

An account of the terrible wounds inflicted on the king during the battle and after his death, along with greater understanding of the cause of his twisted spine, produced a wave of public sympathy for the dead monarch. However, the small treasure which Sheriff Hutton holds had made me sympathetic towards Richard for some time.

It is likely that he was just as tyrannical as any other ruler in the terrible mess that was the Wars of the Roses. The aristocracy suffered financial and political losses but only the occasional execution, while the peasants who fought for them were slaughtered in droves – ten thousand at the Battle of Towton alone. However, something happened to him that every parent dreads. His child died.

Edward of Middleham, Prince of Wales, was born at Middleham Castle and passed away at the age of ten. His burial place is unknown, but a white alabaster cenotaph of a small boy lies in Sheriff Hutton Church. There are arguments about whether this really is where Edward rests, but all I can say is that it feels so to me. This corner of the little church seems hung with sorrow.

Sheriff Hutton Castle

YORKSHIRE WOLDS

When the artist David Hockney left California for East Yorkshire, he drew a line under his sunny American landscapes and took out a box of watercolour paints. Drawn to England by ties of family and a desire for change, he began to paint in a way that was totally different from his earlier work and yet immediately recognizable. Canvases started appearing of tall stands of bare trees, green lanes rutted and dusted with snow, stacked piles of roughly cut logs, and everywhere the huge curve of the Yorkshire sky.

The Wolds are wonderful. Here, in the corner of Yorkshire that reaches down to the Humber estuary and the North Sea, you find a land of chalk downs – a rolling plateau cut through by steep, swerving, often tiny, glacial valleys, and punctuated by tight arching woods of beech.

There's a lightness and sense of restraint in the colours of the land, reflecting the chalk beneath. And a gentleness to the rolling rise and fall of the narrow roads. It's a kind of muted arcadia with small towns and cities – Pocklington, Beverley, Hornsea – twinkling at its edges, and stately homes like ripe fruit – Burton Agnes, Sledmere, Burton Constable – scattered across its acres.

Stand on one of the heights of this landscape – say, beside the monumental Rudston monolith (at 25 feet the tallest standing stone in Britain) – and you will experience a wonderful airy sense of freedom.

Trees by Water

LASTINGHAM

The saints of the early church were fond of finding wild places to bring the word to, and there are a surprisingly large number of churches next to stone circles, monoliths, long barrows and places of dark legends. Lastingham sits in a fold of the hills along the southern side of the North York Moors, and according to Bede, it was a place 'where dragons once lay'. So it's no surprise that St Cedd believed it was the perfect place to found a monastery. Ten years later, in 664, he was an interpreter at the Synod of Whitby and witnessed his beloved Celtic Church forced to cede to the ways of Rome. He died shortly after and was buried at Lastingham.

There were a number of changes in the years to come. When the first stone church of 725 was erected, Cedd was reburied by the altar. In 1078, the Saxon monastery was rebuilt as a Benedictine abbey and a crypt constructed beneath the church over Cedd's grave. In less than ten years, however, the monks, for reasons unknown, left to found the great St Mary's Abbey in York. In time the building became the parish church, decayed, was rebuilt and ended up in its present form in about the fifteenth century.

Arriving in Lastingham is a memorable experience. The road takes you from the barren moors past wind-bent trees before winding downhill, and suddenly you are facing a very old, very beautiful church. Its battlements are almost as high as the encircling hills. Surrounded by the solid stone houses of the small village, the church sits on the great green mound of the graveyard. Inside it feels like a typical country church until you take the stairs which lead down to the crypt. And then, extraordinarily, you are in a church beneath a church.

Massive pillars embellished with carvings support the low roof. The cave of a room is lit by a small window beyond the stone table of the altar. The barrel curve of the vaulting casts dark shadows overhead. This is a space for contemplation.

Lastingham

YORK

It is a thrilling moment when the train from the north curves into York station and the largest Gothic cathedral in northern Europe comes into view. Rising above the ancient grey city walls, its towers echoed by a dozen churches, the Minster is a pale, golden fairytale in stone, set off beautifully against the red brick and blue slate of the houses.

There is so much history in even one street in this place that it's impossible to write about – you will simply have to go and see for yourself. But let me point you to a couple of gems.

Betty's is the ideal café. Sitting within its curved glass walls, which are topped with a stained-glass frieze, feels like reaching the high-water line of civilization. Add a cup of delicious breakfast tea and a dazzling offering from the sweet trolley, and it's hard to see how life could get much better.

But people don't just come here for the tea and cake. Downstairs is a large, very scratched mirror, bearing the signatures of young boys, mostly from Canada, who were stationed near here during the Second World War. North Yorkshire had dozens of airfields from which enormous formations of planes would roar eastward every night; sadly, when they returned in the early morning, their numbers were often much depleted. Relatives would come here regularly to see the mirror and run their fingers over the damaged glass where loved ones, or perhaps their younger selves, had once carved their name.

York station, one of the cornerstones of the railway revolution, is situated just outside the walls of the city. From here lines connected the industrial cities and coalfields of the North with the markets and factories of the South. In York, they made engines, carriages and all the paraphernalia of the railways.

The initial attempt to pull the history of the railways together coherently resulted, rather neatly, from their nationalization in the 1940s. Up till then, all the different railway companies had been keeping their own collections of memorabilia, but in 1951 the first moves towards a national collection began with a museum in Clapham. This was eventually relocated and greatly expanded when the York engine shed and surrounding buildings were turned into the National Railway Museum. It's simply wonderful. And free. It attracts ageing train spotters, Thomas the Tank Engine fans of all ages, and people like me who are enchanted by the gorgeous railway poster designs, which continue to inspire my print making.

York almost became the capital of England. Thank goodness that never happened, for instead of a small, beautiful city with an incomparable collection of churches, houses, pubs and streets, we might have had the concrete shoeboxes of government administration that have blighted the once splendid city of Westminster.

If you've never been, get a train ticket now. It's the only way to arrive.

*Evening
Light, York*

COVERDALE

The first time I came to Coverdale I was driving from Durham to Dow Cave – a pothole in Wharfedale. As I pootled into Wensleydale I worked out that if I took the road over the end of Penhill I could cut off a substantial corner. It turned out to be a good plan, but I doubted its wisdom at first.

My little blue Morris 1000 van, nicknamed the Jellymould, struggled up the near vertical hairpin bends of Capple Bank with a groaning gearbox but finally made it to the highest point of the road. I pulled over and got out.

From here a great swathe of Yorkshire was laid before me. To the left, Wensleydale, with the ridges of Swaledale beyond. Ahead, the Vale of York and the North York Moors. To my right was the undiscovered country of Coverdale, but looking over the grouse-chattering moor I could see a promising line of fells.

I got back into the Morris, crossed the moor and came through a tiny village into a small (by Yorkshire standards) dale of green fields, heather and bracken uplands and limestone farms. Lost in trees in the valley bottom flowed the little River Cover. I turned towards the dale head and my destination.

I've made the journey here dozens of times since and it's always wonderful. As you drive east, Coverdale grows narrower, the hillsides get steeper, the ground more barren. Green hedges become dry stone walls. Driving up the rise to the watershed, the bulk of Great Whernside looms up on the left. Across the moor to the right lie drove roads to Waldendale and Bishopdale. To either side of the cattle grid at the dale head is the Dark Age earthwork of Tor Dyke.

This place is close to paradise. Behind, Coverdale's modest length of 17 miles disappears into the distance. Ahead, the heights of Park Rash fall away into Wharfedale. Above, even in winter, larks seem to sing in a summer sky.

Looking to Great Whernside, Coverdale

BOWES

Nicholas Nickleby is one of the many novels in which Charles Dickens campaigned for change. In this, his third book, he had the abusive practices of a certain type of school in his sights, and as he was researching the story he discovered a perfect real-life villain. Along with his illustrator, the magnificently named Hablot Knight Browne, Dickens travelled to the small town of Bowes in Yorkshire to call on William Shaw, the headmaster of Bowes Academy.

Several schools existed in Westmorland and Yorkshire at this time which promised to educate children for modest fees. However, their true function was to provide a cheap and convenient dumping ground, and pupils were routinely maltreated, starved and beaten. A few years before, William Shaw had been prosecuted for neglect after two children became blind through poor nutrition. And although he cleaned up his act after this, at least one child a year continued to die in his school. He became immortalized in the book as Wackford Squeers, the headmaster of Dotheboys Hall.

While in Bowes, Dickens visited the churchyard to see the graves of deceased pupils, and it was here he conceived the character of Smike, Nicholas's companion.

In contrast to these grim events, Bowes is really a lovely place! Once a coaching town on an ancient route across the Pennines, it has been bypassed by the modern A66 and enjoys a peaceful existence. It is embarrassingly rich in stories, like that of doomed lovers Edwin and Emma in the ballad 'The Pattern of True Love' or 'The Bowes Tragedy', and a hidden treasure under Bowes Castle. Then there is the splendidly creepy tale known as 'The Hand of Glory', which took place on Bowes Moor.

But Wackford Squeers continues to cast a shadow over Bowes's reputation. Dotheboys Hall/Bowes Academy still stands at the west end of the town, and knowing that three hundred boys were once crammed within its modest walls, you can't help imagining some of the horrors perpetrated.

Bowes

RIBBLEHEAD VIADUCT

When I first saw Ribblehead Viaduct it looked fabulous. The massive row of 24 arches marched across Batty Moss, with Whernside to the right and Ingleborough to the left. In the middle of the broken and barren Craven landscape it was a triumphant statement of Victorian engineering. As I got closer, however, the silhouette started to yield up some details and I realized that the slender columns were not as they should be. Baulks of timber and lengths of rusted railway line had been used to bind and reinforce them.

The Settle–Carlisle Railway, one of Britain's most scenic lines, was the subject of a major campaign when closure was threatened in the 1980s, and the focus was this viaduct. It was becoming unsafe and the cost of repairs would be enormous. However, a well-coordinated, passionate group managed to ensure its repair and survival, and now the unsightly reinforcements are gone and the elegant shape of the arches has been restored.

The viaduct took four years to build, between 1870 and 1874, and a hundred of the navvies living in the vast camp on Batty Moss died during that time.

They were handling limestone blocks up to eight tons in weight and laying one and a half million bricks in a place where the wind rarely stops and the cold can be ferocious. The Yorkshire Dales are full of memorable places, each with their distinctive characteristics, but few are as hard and heroic and beautiful as this.

People come here for all sorts of reasons. The fells are honeycombed with potholes, and cavers can explore the limestone passages and caverns while trains gently shake the viaduct above. The Three Peaks Challenge takes place around Ribblehead: an endless stream of walkers, cyclists and fell runners pit themselves against the heights, the elements and the clock to complete the route in the shortest possible time. Film-makers come here – in recent years *Sightseers* and *Lad* have both featured the viaduct. And in their hundreds (and their anoraks), train spot . . . sorry, rail enthusiasts, line the track with their cameras as the *Fellsman* steam train roars majestically by.

The Ribblehead Viaduct symbolizes human ingenuity, the power of protest and the challenges offered by one of England's most breathtaking landscapes. It is a fitting tribute to the Yorkshire Dales.

Ribblehead Viaduct

WHITBY

Whitby has an energetic air about it. There is a freshness, a vivacity, to the town, as though the whole place is just getting ready to put out to sea. Built around a natural harbour on the east coast of Yorkshire, the views are always splendid. It was from here that Captain James Cook set sail and eventually discovered Australia; here that Bram Stoker created the scene in *Dracula* in which the schooner *Demeter*, flying before the gale, comes to rest in the harbour and a great black hound bounds from her lifeless hull. And it was from here that William Scoresby left to explore the Arctic and to unravel the enigma of magnetic north.

But Whitby's first claim to fame is revealed in the ruins of the abbey crowning the East Cliff. St Hilda was an abbess here in the seventh century, and she is remembered in the history books because her monastery was chosen for the Synod of Whitby. (Here took place the great debate about whether the Celtic Church or the Roman Church should prevail.) Locally, her name is attached to the fossilized ammonites, known here as snakestones, found on Whitby's beach. The legend runs that Hilda was faced with a plague of snakes and turned them to stone. Of course, ammonites have no heads, but this little problem was rectified by several Victorian fossil dealers simply carving snake heads on to many of their finds.

The headland of the West Cliff, which rises from the tangle of streets of the old town, is reached by a flight of 199 steps. The church and abbey sail above smokehouses, cottages, chip shops and ships. Whitby has one of the most striking settings of anywhere in Britain.

Whitby

AND IN CONCLUSION

When I started making this book I began with a long list of places, some I had already visited on pilgrimage and some I wanted to explore. However, as I mentioned my ideas to friends and fellow artists, the list grew until I realized that I had only explored the tip of an amazing iceberg. This book and exhibition are simply the beginning of a long journey. I have still many miles to travel and many pictures to make.

If the stories and images here encourage you to go on your own pilgrimages, don't keep it to yourself. Tell others and, if you like, tell me. I'm always looking for new special places to add to the list.

You can email me through my website, which is
<www.ianscottmassie.com>.

ACKNOWLEDGEMENTS

My family has been a huge help in bringing this project to fruition. Josie, my wife, has been to many of these places with me and offered invaluable insights. She has also, heroically, proofread and helped me to find the right shape for what I have wanted to say. My daughter Rosie, an artist, has enthused about a number of places and given me much to think about in how she has portrayed some of these subjects in her own work. My son Paul, a gifted poet, has travelled with me on some of my research trips to share the lovely experiences many of these places have yielded and talk through with me what they feel like.

A number of Facebook and Twitter followers, pupils on my art courses and fellow artists have contributed in a number of ways. I have also been greatly encouraged by the many people who have offered to host the touring exhibition in which the pictures in this book will be displayed.

Last, any errors in the text, stylistic lapses and moments of poor judgement are entirely my responsibility.

SUGGESTED READING

Auden, W. H. 'Roman Wall Blues' in *Another Time* (London: Faber & Faber, 2007)

Betjeman, John (ed.). *Collins Guide to Parish Churches* (London: HarperCollins, revised edition 1993)

Blyth, Ronald, and Smith, Edwin. *Divine Landscapes: A pilgrimage through Britain's sacred places* (London: Viking, 1986)

Causey, Andrew. *Stanley Spencer* (London: Lund Humphries, 2014)

Chaucer, Geoffrey. *The Canterbury Tales*

Dickens, Charles. *Nicholas Nickleby*

Doyle, Arthur Conan. *The Hound of the Baskervilles*

Fox, George. *The Autobiography of George Fox*

Hockney, David. *Hockney's Pictures* (London: Thames & Hudson, 2006)

Housman, A. E. *A Shropshire Lad*

Leber, Michael. *L. S. Lowry* (London: Phaidon Press, 1995)

Lee, Laurie. *Cider with Rosie*

Morley, Paul. *The North: (And almost everything in it)* (London: Bloomsbury, 2014)

Nash, Paul. *Outline: An autobiography* (London: Columbus Books, 1988)

Nash, Paul. *Places* (London: South Bank Centre, 1989)

Norman, Philip. *Shout: The true story of the Beatles* (London: Pan Books, 2003)

Palmer, Simon. *Saltaire: A picture storybook* (Shipley: Salt Estates, 1995)

Peake, Tony, *Derek Jarman: A biography* (London: Abacus, 2001)

Pevsner, Nikolaus. *The Leaves of Southwell* (London: Penguin Books, 1945)

Platt, Colin. *The Traveller's Guide to Medieval England* (London: Martin Secker and Warburg, 1985)

Prebble, John. *Culloden* (London: Pimlico, 2002)

Prebble, John. *The Highland Clearances* (London: Penguin Books, 1982)

Sobel, Dava. *Longitude* (London: HarperCollins, 2005)

Tennyson, Alfred, Lord. *Idylls of the King*

Thomas, Dylan. *Under Milk Wood*

Vaughan, William. *John Constable* (London: Tate Publishing, 2015)

White, T. H. *The Sword in the Stone* (London: HarperCollins, 2008)

White, T. H. *The Once and Future King* (London: HarperCollins, 2015)

Wordsworth, William. *The Collected Poems*

INDEX OF SCREEN PRINTS

INDEX OF WATERCOLOURS

INDEX OF PLACES